MICHAEL FULLAN

The Moral Imperative
REALIZED

A Joint Publication CORWIN
A SAGE Company
 ONTARIO
PRINCIPALS'
COUNCIL
Exemplary Leadership in Public Education

For information:

Corwin
A SAGE Company
2455 Teller Road
Thousand Oaks, California 91320
(800) 233-9936
Fax: (800) 417-2466
www.corwin.com

SAGE India Pvt. Ltd.
B 1/I 1 Mohan Cooperative
   Industrial Area
Mathura Road,
   New Delhi 110 044
India

SAGE Ltd.
1 Oliver's Yard
55 City Road
London EC1Y 1SP
United Kingdom

SAGE Asia-Pacific Pte. Ltd.
33 Pekin Street #02-01
Far East Square
Singapore 048763

Printed in the United States of America

Library of Congress Cataloging-in-Publication Data

Fullan, Michael.
The moral imperative realized/Michael Fullan.
      p. cm.
"A Joint Publication With Ontario Principals' Council."
Includes bibliographical references and index.
ISBN 978-1-4129-9610-5 (pbk.)

   1. School management and organization—United States. 2. Educational leadership—United States. 3. Organizational effectiveness. I. Ontario Principals' Council. II. Title.

LB2805.F848 2011
371.2'012—dc22   2010038189

This book is printed on acid-free paper.

10   11   12   13   14   10   9   8   7   6   5   4   3   2   1

Acquisitions Editor:	Arnis Burvikovs
Associate Editor:	Desirée A. Bartlett
Editorial Assistant:	Kimberly Greenberg
Production Editor:	Melanie Birdsall
Copy Editor:	Sarah J. Duffy
Typesetter:	C&M Digitals (P) Ltd.
Proofreader:	Cheryl Rivard
Indexer:	Sheila Bodell
Cover Designer:	Rose Storey
Permissions Editor:	Karen Ehrmann

The Moral Imperative
REALIZED

Contents

About the Author

Michael Fullan is professor emeritus of the Ontario Institute for Studies in Education of the University of Toronto. Recognized as a worldwide authority on educational reform, Fullan is engaged in advising policymakers and local leaders around the world in helping to achieve the moral purpose of all children learning. His books have been published in many languages.

Fullan is currently Special Advisor to the Premier and Minister of Education in Ontario. His book *Leading in a Culture of Change* was awarded the 2002 Book of the Year Award by Learning Forward (formerly the National Staff Development Council), *Breakthrough* (with Peter Hill and Carmel Crévola) won the 2006 Book of the Year Award from the American Association of Colleges for Teacher Education, *Turnaround Leadership in Higher Education* (with Geoff Scott) won the Bellwether Book Award in 2009, and *Change Wars* (with Andy Hargreaves) was awarded the 2009 Book of the Year Award by Learning Forward. His latest books are *The Six Secrets of Change*, *What's Worth Fighting For in the Principalship*, *Motion Leadership: The Skinny on Becoming Change Savvy*, and *All Systems Go*. He has also just launched a video online learning course called *Motion Leadership the Movie* (Corwin-Sinet).

A list of his widely acclaimed books, articles, and other resources can be found at www.michaelfullan.ca.

Preface

The Moral Imperative Realized is about the actual accomplishment of moral purpose in any endeavor—in this case, for education. It is, in other words, about raising the bar and closing the gap of student achievement for all students—not as a slogan, but as a reality. The moral imperative, of course, has widespread urgency in all areas of human life—in finance, in politics, and in all aspects of how we treat each other. It is at the very heart of the well-being of the individual, the society, and the global world. It is not about religion, but about the purpose and fulfillment of human and social life. Education can lead the way, and, in this book, there will be plenty of named examples of how some educators are already doing so. But it needs to be more widespread in education and in all walks of life. This book tells you what it looks like and how to get more of it.

This is my second book that explicitly addresses the matter of the moral imperative in education. What has changed since I wrote *The Moral Imperative of School Leadership* in 2003? Interestingly, it was that very year—2003—that we began to intensify and deepen our work on the moral imperative. So there is plenty to update. Let's be clear about the topic. In 2003 the concept of moral purpose or moral imperative was fairly new. John Goodlad, in his foreword to *The Moral Imperative of School Leadership,* noted that when he used the term *moral,* people were confused. Was moral purpose about the pure life, religion, the spiritual? For some, this can be the case. But for education reform, it should be clear that the moral imperative focuses on raising the bar and closing the gap in student learning and achievement for *all children regardless of background.* It

x   The Moral Imperative Realized

is about a better society for individuals and for the collective. Not only has this focus become clearer in the last few years, but the moral purpose as we shall see also means being skilled at doing something about it—actually accomplishing greater moral purpose.

There are three big, interrelated developments over the past eight years. First, the idea of moral purpose has become much more serious. There is greater, more intense pressure on making it happen—a growing frustration that more progress is not being made. No Child Left Behind (NCLB) certainly introduced and highlighted the agenda. Its weak suit was its wrong and inadequate strategy to implement moral purpose on any scale. Now we have Race to the Top and related legislation to replace NCLB. There is more intensity—and this time seemingly greater attention to implementation (see Fullan, 2010a). The dramatic new film *Waiting for "Superman,"* by Davis Guggenheim and Lesley Chilcott, shows in gut-wrenching images how the poor in the United States are suffering at the hands of the public education system. There is no question that the stakes are being raised dramatically. The moral imperative is now blasting its way onto front pages across the United States.

Second, we actually know how to accomplish greater moral purpose with results to show for it. I will furnish plenty of cases of actual implementation that allow us to see how it can be put into practice—what I call *realized moral purpose.* We see this in our work under the rubric of *Motion Leadership*—the book (Fullan, 2010b) and the movie (Fullan, 2010c). We will uncover these insights in the chapters that follow.

Third, another dramatic change is that we are addressing larger swaths of the system. No longer is the moral imperative about this or that outstanding school. Rather, it is about whole systems engaged in successful reform—whole districts, whole states or provinces, whole countries. All schools must be implicated in the pursuit of the moral imperative.

This is all good news. Accomplishment, at the end of the day, is always more satisfying than planning. It turns out that school and system leadership are central to this mission. This book zeroes in on school and system leadership to show what it can do on the ground. It reveals how leaders are part and parcel of system change, that they can and must affect the micro and macro pictures. Realizing moral purpose depends on engaged and deeply committed leaders at all levels of the system.

There are four chapters in this book. The first makes clear that moral purpose by itself is not a strategy. If you do not know how to implement moral purpose, you really don't have it. And if you are passionate about it and others don't get it, you still don't have it. If you whip people into a frenzy and have no viable strategy to go forward, you are once again setting up the poor for failure. Action in the early stages is messy, but leaders with effective moral purpose persist and figure it out. This book both shows what success looks like and helps guide the way to do more of it—more of it on a dramatic, large scale.

The second chapter takes us inside success as we look at realized moral purpose. Not only do we have more clear examples of how to go from failure to success, there is greater specificity and precision about how to get there. The core components, the smallest number of key factors required for success, are increasingly known. And they are small in number. These elements of success must be pursued relentlessly and in concert, but they are not a mystery any longer—tough work, but doable, and oh so satisfying and energizing.

The third chapter links the school and the district, demonstrating clearly that the success of principals and that of the district are closely intertwined. Indeed, the success of peers among peers is crucial. I will show that building up school-to-school allegiance and friendly competition are powerful ways to improve many schools simultaneously.

The final chapter examines the increasingly visible presence of system leaders in action, but it is eminently practical and grounded (as well as uplifting). All in all, the work of school leaders is becoming more meaningful, more exciting, and above all more central to the success of education systems in any country. For those who wanted purpose and those who wanted action, you can now find it in one place—the school of the 21st century, nested in education systems that treat education success and societal success as deeply symbiotic. Leadership, a phenomenon that has been everything and nothing, has finally found its niche. It is clear, powerful, challenging, frustrating, and deeply morally fulfilling. As we found in *Motion Leadership*, practice drives practice. There is no better driver than realizing one's moral purpose.

Acknowledgments

I would like to thank the editorial team at Corwin—Arnis Burvikovs, Melanie Birdsall, and Sarah Duffy. They keep getting better and better—a productive joy to work with. And thanks to the Ontario Principals' Council, who are co-publishers of most of my books. OPC continues to be a huge force for realized moral purpose.

Thanks also to Curtis Linton and the crew at School Improvement Network PD 360®, to Mark German and others at Corwin, and to our own Claudia Cuttress for the fantastic and exciting journey in producing *Motion Leadership the Movie*. We found many, many examples of "moral purpose realized" in the six districts, one state, and one province that we filmed—great accomplishments that lead to even more. Realization is its own driver.

It is well to think well. It is divine to act well.

—Horace Mann

CHAPTER ONE

Moral Purpose Is Not a Strategy

W*aiting for "Superman"* (www.waitingforsuperman .com) is a powerful film directed by Davis Guggenheim (2010) and produced by Lesley Chilcott, of *An Inconvenient Truth* fame. Among other things, it shows specific promises from every president since Lyndon Johnson about education being the central priority, whether it be the Elementary and Secondary Education Act of 1965, or Goals 2000 in 1989, or No Child Left Behind of 2001, or Race to the Top in 2010.

Each president fervently commits himself and the government to addressing the crisis of education. Fast-forward to 2011. The United States has slipped from first in the world in high school graduation and university participation to about 24th. It has tripled its per-pupil expenditures in constant dollars to become the biggest spender on education in the world. And the life chances of the poor have become deeply mired in the muck of failed reform after failed reform. In most large urban cities with race and poverty tag-teaming to hold people down, children and youth know more people personally who are in jail than who are in postsecondary education. Prison enrollment, so to speak, has exploded at a cost of $35,000 per inmate, while school enrolment limps along at $10,000 per pupil, itself the highest in the world.

Waiting for "Superman" is a disturbing portrayal, even at the macro level. But it gets gut-wrenching when it follows the fortunes of five poor kids—Anthony and Bianca (black), Daisy and Francisco (mixed), and Emily (white)—as their parents (mostly single moms) struggle to get their children in charter schools with strong quality reputations. These schools admit children using a lottery system with anywhere from a 1-in-5 to a 1-in-20 chance of being selected. Only Emily gets selected, and Anthony is admitted later from a waiting list. The personal heartbreak is horrible. The system that forces kids and their parents to struggle through the agony (for the large majority) of hopes rising and being dashed is wicked. That hope would be reduced to providing escape routes for a few children is morally reprehensible and socially irresponsible. That is the message of the film's producers as well. Unfortunately, they fall short on furnishing even a directional solution.

Waiting for "Superman" captures the moral imperative writ large, and writ deep. But in my view, this is not the moral *imperative* if only a handful of disadvantaged kids get a chance. The first two-thirds of the film is as brilliant as it is alarming. Unfortunately, the last third relies on moral outrage as its sole strategy and fails to identify any way out other than to say we need more schools with passionate leaders and teachers. Of course we do. But moral purpose, even deeply felt, by itself is not a strategy. We need moral purpose actualized, and on a very large scale. The latter is the essence of this book.

MORAL IMPERATIVE AS STRATEGY

So the question is not just how deep is your moral imperative, but equally, what is your strategy to enact it. Just as moral imperative is not a strategy, neither is being "right." We will see the strategies in detail, especially in Chapters 2 and 3, but let's establish some basics here for making the moral imperative a strategy (see Exhibit 1.1).

Exhibit 1.1 Moral Imperative as Strategy

1. Make a personal commitment
2. Build relationships
3. Focus on implementation
4. Develop the collaborative
5. Connect to the outside
6. Be relentless (and divert distracters)

Make a Personal Commitment

Although, as we shall see, not every principal needs to be a martyr, not a bad place to start is George Bernard Shaw:

> I want to be thoroughly used up when I die, for the harder I work, the more I live. I rejoice in life for its own sake. Life is no "brief candle" to me. It is a sort of splendid torch which I have got hold of for the moment, and I want to make it burn as brightly as possible before handing it on to future generations.

A bit overstated for our purpose, but it gets us in the mood. School leadership is serious business. It takes a combination of clear personal values, persistence against a lot of odds, emotional intelligence, thick skin, and resilience. It also takes a knack for focusing on the right things and for problem solving. We will see plenty of named cases of this in action, but let us realize that the best leaders have strong values and are skilled at strategy. Attila the Hun and Hitler meet this definition. Leaders with moral purpose, on the other hand, have a different content—deep commitment to raising the bar and closing the gap for all students.

Leaders need to support, activate, extract, and galvanize the moral commitment that is in the vast majority of teachers. Most teachers want to make a difference, and they especially like leaders who help them and their colleagues achieve success in terrible circumstances. Revealingly, once this process is under way, teachers as a group value leaders who help the hardcore resistant teachers leave. When this happens, the cohesion of the rest of the staff actually *increases* (Bryk, Bender Sebring, Allensworth, Luppescu, & Easton, 2010; Linton, 2011).

At the individual teacher level, the equation is depicted in Exhibit 1.2.

Yes, the passion, purpose, and capacity of teachers in the service of students is the key, but how does one enact these qualities if they are weak or missing? How does one realize them on a very large scale? The school leaders' new niche is exactly this work. You can't get blood out of a stone, but the leaders you will encounter in this book do get blood out of things that look like stones. Moral imperative realized is the bottom line.

There is a pretty hefty tome, *Moral Clarity: A Guide for Grown-Up Idealists,* by Susan Neiman (2009), that I would not recommend that you read from cover to cover, but there is one key message that comes through loud and clear: Don't expect to find moral purpose somewhere other than in yourself. However much you are inspired by other people's examples or by the written word, "you are responsible for thinking it

Exhibit 1.2	Teacher Passion, Purpose, and Capacity Equated to Student Engagement and Learning

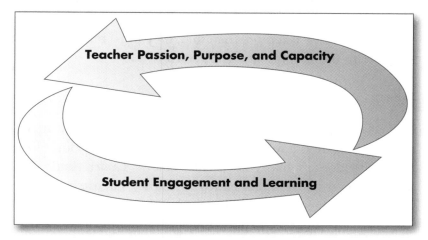

Source: Adapted from Fullan, 2003.

through on your own" (p. 18). And this is not a one-time proposition: "Moral judgment is not a matter of decisions made once and for all, but of keeping your eye on distinctions" (p. 3).

Clarity of purpose is a crucial foundation, but how you get there is craft. As Neiman (2009) puts it, "creating moral order in the world is just what we're meant to give back to it. If there is going to be reason in the world, it is we who have to put it there" (p. 429). In other words, we are on our own (but as we shall see, we can get plenty of help from others).

Finally, I should say that personal commitment must be accompanied by optimism that progress can be made even in the most troubled situations. Without that we are done before we start. Take Neiman's (2009) wisdom on the matter: "Nothing promotes inertia like cynicism" (p. 77). Or, more fully: "Cynicism punctures the energy that leads you to try. It suggests that you know it all, so your action is always *Yeah?*

So, what else is new? Once you start saying that you'll allow anything to happen" (p. 401, italics in original).

School leaders, then, must come to have what I call *informed optimism* (we solved the last problem, so we can figure out this one). But more than that, they must build relationships with the skeptics and the cynics.

Build Relationships

I once observed, only half-facetiously, that emotional intelligence is building a relationship with someone you don't like, and who doesn't like you. In *The Change Leader* (Fullan, in press), I have a few "killer slides" (insights that are especially powerful). The one that fits here is "All effective leaders combine resolute moral purpose with impressive empathy." We already know about resolute moral purpose—the necessary but not sufficient drive to keep going even when things are not working. But to get anywhere you have to build relationships with many different people—people who disagree with you, the skeptical and cynical. If you are to have any chance of progressing, you have to have enough empathy for their situation so that you can relate to them. It is impressive because they are slowing you down, so to speak. It is impressive because you understand their perspective even if it is not yours.

In some toxic situations, you need to get rid of some people, but normally you will need to build relationships with diverse people. In motion leadership, we pay a lot of attention to sequence. The rule of thumb here is that if you want to challenge someone to do better, you'd better build a relationship first. So all this talk about relationships being crucial is correct. But you have to realize it as part and parcel of the moral imperative in action.

This is very specific work. Take Yarrow's (2009) recent survey of the state of mind of teachers in the United States. He

found that 40% are *disheartened*, 23% *idealists*, and 37% co
tented. We can quibble with the purity of the labels (some c.
the disheartened are surely cynical), but we can see immediately that the principal must relate to all three groups. For the
disheartened, the principal will need to help them realize
moral purpose, thereby stirring their motivation to get engaged
(see Chapter 2). For the idealists, it may be a matter of appre-
ciating them and helping them work with others who are not
so motivated. The contented will need to be galvanized into
action. Incidentally, one of the most important working conditions that teachers always cite is having a good principal.

As leaders, then, we can't depend on encountering teachers or parents or students who are already optimistic that success is possible. Some teachers need to go, but the majority in
difficult circumstances will have to be convinced through new
experiences that progress is possible. Indeed, leaders have to
help people taste success that they never have experienced
before.

We will see specific, even dramatic examples in subsequent chapters, but let me portray the mindset of the moral
imperative. Some of these words will sound odd, but here is
the essence:

1. Leaders facing terrible situations will have to lead with
   respect. Put differently, they will have to convey respect
   before people have earned it.

2. Leaders need to do everything possible to create conditions that make people lovable (mainly by creating circumstances that favor success).

3. And then leaders must deal firmly with what's
   left over.

It is not as simple as *1, 2, 3,* but realized moral purpose is
just what it says. You actually accomplish results. Nothing
else counts. And when you do get somewhere, the energy that

is released enables the group to go places they never thought possible. Once they experience that, they will never go back.

Focus on Implementation

In all of our work at the school, district, and state levels, there is one factor that stands out time and again when it comes to success—and the word is _focus._ Doug Reeves (in press) has written a book about it, _Finding Your Leadership Focus._ He shows that most leaders fall victim to the "law of initiative fatigue." Too many ad hoc piecemeal initiatives descend on school leaders, and some leaders add insult to injury by voluntarily pursuing too many projects and innovations. Instead, argues Reeves, leaders must concentrate on a cluster of three essential practices: focus, monitoring in relation to the focus, and displaying a strong sense of efficacy. A sense of efficacy is not so much advance confidence that you can succeed but rather that you can make things work, that what you have to do is within your control. Efficacy is very close to realized purpose because it stems from your experience that you can be successful. It may be a huge struggle, but you, working with others, will get there.

The focus I am talking about must be on instructional practice. In Ontario, we have had widespread success in substantially improving literacy and numeracy in over 5,000 schools by focusing on these priorities and by going deep in assessment and improvement of teaching and learning geared to the individual needs of the students teachers have before them (Fullan, 2010a). The moral imperative needs to be channeled into the improvement of practice. You see it time and again in the works of Reeves, Elmore, DuFour, and many others. The moral imperative, deep focus, constructive monitoring, and corresponding efficacious action are an unstoppable combination.

Develop the Collaborative

Effective leaders with moral purpose don't do it alone. And they don't do it by hiring and supporting "individuals." Instead, they develop and employ the collaborative. Time and again we see the power of collective capacity. When the group is mobilized with focus and specificity, it can accomplish amazing results (what we call in motion leadership *the speed of quality implementation*). The collaborative, sometimes known as professional learning communities, gets these results because not only are leaders being influential, but peers are supporting and pressuring each other to do better.

This collective capacity is the sine qua non of whole-system reform. It gets built up within the school, but also is fostered as schools learn from each other. Focused groups large and small are unequivocally more productive. The moral imperative is a distinctively social enterprise.

Connect to the Outside

The power of the collaborative is seen not only within schools but also in networks, clusters, or other means of deliberately using well-led peer learning strategies. Again, we will see specific examples later. Connecting to the outside is essential for the moral imperative to have sufficient infrastructure. In fact, a principal's moral imperative is stunted if it is only applied internally to that specific school (see Chapter 3).

Of course, the outside is big and we will have to differentiate. The outside will include other schools in your district, parents and community, the district itself, and the larger state and national context. The moral imperative is systemic.

Be Relentless (and Divert Distracters)

Maggie Jackson (2009), in *Distracted*, shows in frightening detail how our ability to focus is being systematically eroded by the frenetic pace of modern life, with its myriad technology and related fragmented bits and bytes. She says, "We are less and less able to see, hear, and comprehend what's relevant and permanent . . . so many of us feel that we can barely keep our head above water, and our days are marked by perpetual loose ends" (p. 14). Sounds like the job description of the 21st-century school principal!

Jackson (2009) recommends that we cultivate a renaissance of focus, judgment, and awareness. Paying attention on a sustained basis to what is and might be important is extremely difficult under today's conditions, and there can be no better example than the current principalship. I will show specific named examples to demonstrate that effective principals cultivate their resolute moral purpose, and they do so by being exquisitely aware of the distractions and diversions on the way. They work both sides of the coin simultaneously—they stay the course on key priorities, and they proactively blunt or divert what might get in the way.

Interestingly, not all the distracters are bureaucratic or imposed. As indicated earlier by Doug Reeves, ad hoc innovations and initiatives—each of which makes sense in its own independent way—can be just as diluting. Thus we need to think of focus and coherence together—coherent focus, relentlessly pursued—while paying attention to data, especially that which is related to individual student progress and to the motivation of adults who can do something to further achievement.

MORAL PURPOSE IS NOT SUFFICIENT

I have said that there is more to moral purpose than moral purpose. The moral imperative to be realized must combine deep commitment and the means of enacting it. Thus *commitment plus strategy* are required. If either commitment or strategy is weak, the result is failure.

Let's consider some examples from Bryk and Schneider's (2002) work in Chicago. Their Ridgeway Elementary School is a good case in point. The principal, Dr. Newman, articulates a strong philosophy of "students as his first priority" and staff as a close second. The authors elaborate:

> Dr. Newman knew that he needed to establish trusting relationships with all members of his school community to advance its improvement efforts. He was articulate about what this meant to him. "Trust is built by contact, by consistency, by doing what you say you're going to do, by showing concern, by acting on solutions, [but] mostly by doing what you say you're going to do." Throughout our interviews, Dr. Newman talked at length about the importance of positive social relations in the functioning of a good school, and felt strongly that developing trust was critical within his school community. (pp. 38–39)

Despite this attractive philosophy, Dr. Newman, in practice, attempted to be conciliatory with individuals and groups. Far from Collins's (2001) "disciplined thought and action" in "confronting the brutal facts" (p. 13) with respect to performance, the principal pushed a little but backed off in the face of any opposition. Conflict avoidance in the face of poor performance is an act of moral neglect. Bryk and Schneider (2002) make a number of observations:

- Relational trust atrophies when individuals perceive that others are not acting in ways that are consistent with their understandings of the other's role obligations. (p. 51)
- Although the principal appeared to listen to everyone's concerns, he rarely followed up on them. (p. 51)

- The stronger teachers at Ridgeway limited their interactions with other staff who they regarded as behaving unprofessionally toward their students. (p. 51)
- Absent a base of collegial trust, a few individual teachers might attempt some innovations in their own classrooms, but larger initiatives that demanded coordinated effort would remain unsuccessful. (p. 52)
- Dr. Newman's seeming willingness to tolerate both incompetence and a lack of commitment within the faculty undermined his relational trust with parents, community leaders, and his own teachers. (p. 53)

Seems like a fairly straightforward case of lack of integrity and courage until you find out that many teachers didn't mind the laissez-faire approach—they preferred to be left alone. (The moral imperative is decidedly *not* leaving people alone; revealingly, people like autonomy when they experience bad bosses and poor peers [Fullan, in press].) When it came time to renew the principal's contract (a responsibility of the school's Local School Council [LSC] in Chicago's relatively decentralized system at the time), Bryk and Schneider (2002) report the following:

> Many teachers attended the LSC meeting. . . . One teacher . . . voiced strong support for Dr. Newman. She spoke of Ridgeway as a "professional environment" and described Dr. Newman as a "very visible principal" who is compassionate and "caring" [and that] "it would be a big loss to the community if Dr. Newman does not remain at Ridgeway." (p. 43)

Two months later the LSC voted, "with a noticeable lack of enthusiasm" (p. 43), to renew Dr. Newman's contract. Moral purpose on the surface is not the moral imperative.

Bryk and Schneider (2002) offer another example, this time a principal with an apparently stronger moral purpose,

but who also ended up accomplishing little. The principal at
Thomas Elementary School in Chicago is Dr. Gonzalez. On
arriving at the school, "he spoke passionately" about the ties
between home and school:

> I would say that Chicago School Reform provides the
> opportunity for society to define a specific school that
> fits some kind of common values—a place that will be
> called the neighborhood school in which the values of
> the home and school are going to be similar. It is amaz-
> ing to me how much discontinuity exists between the
> school values and the home values. Especially in the
> inner-city schools, you definitely find that there is a tre-
> mendous gap. For me, that is one of the basic reasons
> for school failure, the tremendous gap that exists
> between the school and parents. (p. 56)

Fundamental change was required at Thomas Elementary
School. The principal attempted this by working with teachers
as he fostered relations with the community. Again, on the
surface it looked like a winning combination:

> Strong principal leadership was needed to bring this
> faculty together. Dr. Gonzalez came to Thomas School
> as reform began. He articulated a vision for Thomas as
> a responsive institution to its local community. He
> sought to strengthen the role of parents in the educa-
> tion of their own children and demonstrated his per-
> sonal regard for them through his day-to-day efforts at
> the school and around the neighborhood. He also rec-
> ognized the importance of building a professional com-
> munity among his teachers, and dedicated resources
> for their professional development (which was relatively
> uncommon in the early 1990s in Chicago). In many
> ways, Dr. Gonzalez offered a very appealing vision for

both teachers and parents at Thomas School. Nonetheless, reform never really came together at Thomas during our three years of fieldwork there. (Bryk & Schneider, 2002, pp. 71–72)

As Dr. Gonzalez pushed forward with reform, which included bilingualism (given a largely Hispanic clientele) and literacy improvement, he was unable to reconcile the conflict accompanying the changes with the trust and support essential for staying the course. As tensions rose, he "responded by taking a low-key approach" (Bryk & Schneider, 2002, p. 72). Once again we see vision-driven change that sounds good but fails to go much below the surface.

There are countless other examples of failed moral purpose documented in the literature. But that is not the point of this book. I am much more interested in actual success and how to get there. We will see, in the next two chapters, many named examples of moral purpose realized in Canada and the United States. The good news, although it is not nearly widespread enough, is that some systems have figured out that it is essential to go from slogan to sleuthing, and from sleuthing to success.

One last point that will become evident in the next chapter: Effective principals with moral purpose are not successful because they got everyone onboard in advance. The secret to *how* is the realization that success is created by a process that builds capacity and ownership through cumulative learning and commitment (see Fullan, 2010b). Strangely enough, advance agreement about a new direction bears no necessary relationship to the quality of subsequent implementation. And advance disagreement is not fatal. The moral imperative can be rescued or, if you like, created by good leaders during the process of implementation.

Remember Killer Slide No. 1: Effective leaders combine resolute moral purpose with impressive empathy.

It's all about realization.

CHAPTER TWO

Realized Moral Purpose

H ere is a second "killer slide" and a powerful new insight: "What energizes educators is *realized* moral purpose." In other words, if you are a teacher in a struggling school, it is not greater moral exhortation or reams of irrefutable data that are going to motivate you (for one thing, they don't tell you how); rather, it is leaders and peers who actually help you get, or realize, results in your situation. In this chapter, I furnish named case examples showing that even the deadliest cultures can be turned to high energy and success by combining moral resoluteness and focused change strategy. I take four examples from our work in Ontario; 100 examples, so to speak, from Tony Bryk and colleagues' new work; and three more briefly from the work of Rick DuFour, Becky DuFour, Bob Eaker, and Gayle Karhanek's recent book.

The key issue, as I have said, is not so much what success looks like but how to get it if you don't have it. The power of the moral imperative is partly as an advance driver, but largely as a renewed energizer once you start to get somewhere. For the average teachers, achieving moral purpose is why they came into teaching in the first place. Collective achievement under terribly challenging circumstances can activate the most dormant moral purpose and even, I daresay, *create* moral purpose that wasn't there.

Before delving into the bigger cases, let's consider two small-scale vignettes of what moral purpose realized feels like up close when it happens. I take two examples from my experience in Ontario pursuing the moral imperative on a system-wide basis. One example is about a high school student, the other about a teacher who discovered, to her joy (and then to her horror when she realized how she had failed her previous students), that she could make a difference with students whom she had seen as not capable of good work. The moral imperative realized is truly heart-blowing.

Cassandra was a 19-year-old dropout in Ontario when she wandered back to her school. Little did she know that the "system" in the meantime had made some changes to serve all students—raise the bar and close the gap. Here in her own words, and with her permission, is her story.

My name is Cassandra Costa. I am a graduating student at Monsignor Fraser College, Norfinch Campus. I arrived at Msgr. Fraser Norfinch in September 2008. I was a high school dropout for two years and not even sure if I was ready enough to return to school. I remember very clearly the first day when I nervously walked into the guidance counsellor's office and discovered that I was eligible to participate in a co-op program called the OPS Learn and Work. Little did I know then the impact that this program would have in my life.

Almost two years have passed since that first day at Fraser when I only had eight credits to my transcript. I was 17 years old then, with no sense of future—no purpose, goals, or even a care about myself. I simply and even blindly started school to see if I had even a chance at getting my high school diploma.

What motivated me to attend my OPS school classes was the fact that I began to feel like I was part of something meaningful. In those early days, I was impressed about how much there was to learn about the working world and what I needed to be successful in it. I learned about Essential Skills, and while I did not understand what they meant and even what·they were used for, I knew that they would somehow help me grow and understand what I needed to move on with my life—at least that's what Ms. Joyce kept saying over and over again. Yes, Ms. Joyce, I understand them now and, boy, are they ever important.

My first placement was at the Ontario Science Centre. When I was told that I was going there, I clearly remember the fear and anxiety that came over me. My first thought was, "OMG the government hates me. Me plus science equals explosion." At that moment, I felt that I was not even worthy of being around such educated people like the ones I imagined at the Science Centre with all those letters after their names. My time at the Science Centre, however, was incredible! Karen Hager, my manager; Sarah Porrie, my workplace buddy; and the whole department made me feel so special and part of the team. I learned that I was able to do things that I never thought I could do. And those darn Essential Skills—I had to use them! Little did I know, I had some of them already and everyone at the Centre to enable me to enhance them. The highlight of my experience there was my involvement in a project for an event related to the International Year of Astronomy. Astronomy? I only knew that the word was related to stars. By the end of this experience, though, not only did I have a better understanding of the term,

I was given an opportunity to explore it and then even design my own 3D PowerPoint slide show. My work was displayed in a studio and showed Science Centre visitors the meaning of words like *constellations, planets*, and our beautiful undiscovered universe. WOW! Me plus science now equals personal success and growth.

My second placement was at Delisle Youth Services. Here I go again, the government hates me. But once again, I was wrong. Delisle was so much more. With the support of Christine Miranda, my manager, and my workplace buddy, Arc-angela, I learned that my age is not entirely a true reflection of who I am, but my personality is. At Delisle, I was able to use different Essential Skills to engage myself in assisting young adults through the publication of a magazine. Now, I am Cassandra Costa, a publisher!

So my year as an OPS Learn and Work Student came to an end in June of 2009. I earned eight credits in this program. At night school, I pocketed two more and even recovered two others. Now, 12 credits were earned in one school year. What's even better, I took part in the OPS Learn and Work Transition Summer School program and earned another two. WOW, now I am up to 14 credits in one calendar year! Yes, I learned my numeracy skills well, Ms. Joyce.

This past year, I have been in the regular school program at Fraser and continued to earn credits at night school. I also have not left the Ontario Public Service. Me, Cassandra Costa, remains an employee at her once Learn and Work Co-op Placements. I was offered part-time work at both locations and have worked continuously since last summer. I am now a visitor experience host at the Science Centre and a team member of a Youth Engagement Project at Delisle Youth Services. Best of all, I will soon be a high school graduate—earning a total credit count of 30. On June 29, 2010, Cassandra Costa, with all of her Essential Skills, will be an Ontario Secondary School Diploma recipient. That chance to graduate almost two years ago has been made possible by the OPS Learn and Work Program. Thank you so much for providing students like me with this most amazing opportunity.

There have been at least 20,000 teenagers "rescued" in the past seven years in Ontario because of the *enacted* moral purpose of system leaders (see Fullan, 2010a). But the story is deep, disturbing, and ultimately uplifting when you realize the multiplier effect (for better or for worse) of individual teachers. Some teachers don't realize their moral purpose until they are helped to know what they don't know, as shown in the following vignette by Mary Jean Gallagher, the chief student achievement officer and head of the Learning Secretariat in Ontario.

Ontario has now experienced several years of improved learning by our students. As we work to assist the remaining students who are working at Level 2 in their acquisition of higher-level thinking skills, our work requires increasingly precise teaching. One way we are fostering this is through the Teaching Learning Critical Pathway. Teachers come together at least three times in a six-week cycle to plan together and to examine student work. At the beginning of the cycle, they assess their students' work and identify the level to which they believe they can raise each student's skills over the six weeks. They then implement their teaching plans and meet mid-cycle to compare progress, challenges, and potential approaches. At the end they meet and assess their students' performance again. Invariably, most students' performance at the end of the cycle far exceeds that which their teachers predicted. This is a powerful lesson in teacher efficacy and can be very emotional.

At one such closing session, one Grade 4 teacher came to the microphone in tears: "I came to these PD [professional development] sessions because my principal sent me, saying she needed some staff to attend. At the first session I knew I should not have come. I looked at examples of Grade 4 student work from other teachers and I felt really badly—I had been teaching for years and knew my students could never produce such high-quality writing. I did my best, though, to follow the process, feeling sick at heart for my kids. As the cycle progressed, my classroom soared." Here the tears flowed in earnest: "Every one of my kids has produced writing at the high end of Level 3, some at Level 4. They have all doubled and tripled the gains I predicted. For 25 years of teaching, I have set our goals too low. How many more of my students could have reached so much higher if only I had known I could take them there?"

This example vividly conveys that moral purpose without experiencing success is empty. Realization, on the other hand, makes teachers soar because they know *how* to get success, and thus they know it can be done. They become, whenever it happens at any stage of their career, the moral agents of change that drew them to teaching in the first place.

ONTARIO: CROSBY, ARMADALE, RIDEAU, SOUTH SIMCOE

Crosby Heights Public School, Armadale Public School, Rideau Elementary School, and South Simcoe Public School are prime examples of bad or stagnant cultures becoming enlivened through moral leadership and change savvy (see Dean, in press, for more information on South Simcoe; Sharratt & Fullan, 2009, with respect to Crosby Heights and Armadale). The results are dramatic.

Although I focus on the school level in this chapter, it is important to know that each of these schools is nested in a district that is actively promoting systemwide reform in all of its schools. York Region has become one of the highest-performing districts in Ontario (see Sharratt & Fullan, 2009). Another district, Durham, which houses South Simcoe, won the Bertlesmann prize for being a highly innovative district in a worldwide competition. These districts are diverse and have challenging circumstances. But they do better than others because they combine a moral imperative with a comprehensive, focused deep strategy to enact it on a continuous basis for all their schools.

Crosby Heights is a K–8 school of 662 students in a low-income neighborhood in a growing York Region community just north of Toronto, Ontario. It was designated by the district as a Performance Plus School over the years, that is, a school in challenging circumstances requiring attention. After three years of focused work, the principal, Ryan Friedman, and his team have produced phenomenal results. Reading, writing, and math scores on the province's high-standard measures have virtually doubled from an average low of 43% to a high of 83%—a mind-blowing accomplishment, but not a mystery. What was the starting point, and what did the leadership do to overcome the entrenched negative culture?

Ryan Friedman was appointed as school principal at Crosby in 2004. This is what he inherited in the school:

- No clear vision or focal point
- A toxic, negative culture
- A shabby, dilapidated building

- A culture of union–management conflict
- Parents who wanted to move their children to other schools
- An unsafe school environment
- Lack of common language regarding instruction
- Low student achievement results on provincial assessments

I stated in the previous chapter that building relationships when they are negative or weak is a leader's first priority. Effective leaders with moral purpose do this by being clear about their values while honoring the process of change. Ryan stated up front his five nuggets:

1. Learning for all, whatever it takes

2. All equals *all*

3. Students and staff can articulate their potential

4. A focus on balanced literacy

5. Excellence in all that we do

While, like all good leaders, he constantly reiterated and modeled these core values, he was also sensitive about the process. With the union leaders (the district's union president was on his staff), Ryan said that he considered the collective agreement to be "our" agreement (after all, it is a "collective" agreement). For example, he committed to having collaborative time for teachers "between the bells" as he put it, not after school.

Ryan then set about to model, share, and guide practice focusing on literacy. He was patient but persistent. He used several strategies to change beliefs and understandings (following another motion leadership principle: behaviors change before beliefs). Among the strategies he used were the following:

1. Establish job-embedded learning within the school as a route to creating a professional learning culture.

2. Build relationships with teachers, support staff, and students through constant personal interaction.

3. Transfer a few teachers who struggled to buy into the basic moral purpose. (This was a large school and only a few left.)

4. Have high expectations of teachers to engage in assessment and instruction.

5. Provide needed resources for teachers, including getting additional resources.

6. Model hope, optimism, lifelong learning, and caring for others.

7. Celebrate small, incremental successes.

8. Put in place multiple teams to distribute the leadership and to accept responsibility for teacher practice and student improvement.

There is widespread agreement that the school is immensely a better place three years later, and the results speak for themselves. Two quotes, one from a new teacher, and the other from a longtime teacher, provide richer detail.

Ryan does an excellent job of promoting and reinforcing a shared sense of purpose. He uses data to inform us of progress toward our goal, sends articles to read to enhance our PD [professional development], and lets us know about district workshops that we may want to attend. He is very approachable and easy to talk to about issues, concerns, or questions that I have as a first-year teacher. His caring about the needs of his staff is greatly appreciated and admired. He trusts us as educators. When he feels strongly about an issue, he is very diplomatic in his delivery of his point of view, which contributes to his respect of others. (New teacher)

He is consistently approachable and visible within the school. He works hard to resolve conflicts and build good relationships with staff and students. He is respectful of others, as demonstrated in his mannerisms, language, and actions. He encourages teachers to take on new leadership roles, involves community and family participation in the school, and most definitely demonstrates a deep knowledge of teaching and the learning process. I admire the fact that he is constantly willing to learn new things and share what he has learned with others. His use of data to drive instruction has helped us all see that this is an important tool. He has built consensus around the school plan and delivers on his commitments. He has made a significant change in our school and made it such a positive place to be. (Veteran teacher)

We see here the moral imperative at its best—unwavering but respectful; unapologetically forthright but approachable; focused (on the goal and the practices to achieve it); sensitive to building capacity, leadership in others; and celebrating success as a collective accomplishment.

Jill Maar is principal of Armadale Public School, also in York Region and also a large multicultural school, with 890 students and 67 staff. When Jill arrived as principal in 2008, the school was stagnant. Not a negative culture as in Crosby, but definitely going nowhere. The building was ill kept; the norm was one of quietly going about your own business; student achievement was low, hovering around 55%, well below the district average; and parent and community participation from the largely Tamil population was limited.

Fast-forward 12 months, and the number of students at risk substantially declined from 378 to 233 (still a large number, but remember, this is only 12 months of work); attendance at family-community-school events climbed by 200%; and student achievement in literacy and numeracy jumped 19%, virtually reaching the district average.

The strategies Jill used are not all that different from what Ryan did except for contextual nuances. (All good principals are similar in what they focus on and do.) Jill and her school leadership team developed and implemented a plan of action based on the following components:

1. Improve the learning conditions: clean, organized, bright, well-lit plant.

2. Organize, increase, and give access to resources geared to instructional goals.

3. Centralize and streamline budget decisions; develop a clear, transparent process to address essential needs.

4. Examine data and identify trends; reshape teacher thinking about the importance of data when making instructional decisions (e.g., at-risk identification, case management approach).

5. Engage district curriculum consultant experts; facilitate professional learning based on teacher need, and ensure consistency of practice within and across grades.

6. Strategically build a leadership team; support implementation and share practices that work.

7. Renew focus on parent and family engagement: extended library hours, parent/family town hall sessions, street festivals, and heritage and English language classes.

8. Attend to early and ongoing interventions; kindergarten/ Grade 1 programs focus on oral language and use of the

Reading Recovery Observation Survey as a valuable assessment tool to guide instruction.

9. Hold your nerve: protecting instructional time, honoring the literacy block, and designating specific time to meet in school to discuss program needs and students' increased literacy achievement.

Jill is a dedicated instructional leader. She represents focus, focus, focus. She stays the course. She supports teachers and has high expectations. She takes all excuses off the table. She celebrates success as a result of the collective effort of teachers, students, support staff, custodians, and parents.

Third is Rideau Elementary School, in Limestone District School Board, in Eastern Ontario—a school that Ben Levin (2008) visited when he was deputy minister of education. Here is a school with "ordinary teachers," a school with over 300 high-need students. When it began three years ago on the improvement path, the school had fewer than 20% of its students reaching the provincial standard in sixth-grade reading. At the beginning, few teachers believed that their particular students were capable of dramatic improvement. They also felt that a large number of behavior issues and students' personal problems would have to be addressed before reading could be taught.

Three years later with these same students and the same staff, you find 70% of the school's sixth-grade students meeting the provincial standard. The teachers, says Levin (2008), are fiercely proud of what they have achieved. Basically, with focused leadership internal and external (literacy coach) to the school, they zeroed in on effective instructional reading practices. The principal and teachers learned new teaching practices together. (Another key finding on the role of the principal: The one factor that stands out as twice as powerful as any other factor with respect to the principal's impact on student outcomes is the extent to which he or she *participates as a learner* in helping teachers figure out how to improve instruction.)

The teachers "owned these new practices"; they said they would never go back to their old ways, and they realized that if they could do it,"any school could do it" (Levin, 2008, p. 108). What seemed impossible at the beginning was not all that hard in retrospect, and oh so exhilarating.

But this realization is also deeply disturbing, as we saw earlier in Mary Jean Gallagher's vignette. There is joy when teachers discover that they can achieve success in situations that they previously experienced as mostly hopeless. And then there is guilt that all those years went by when they didn't know what they didn't know, and students whose life chances could have been dramatically different failed.

Then the new day, the rest of the career, becomes wildly exciting and energizing when these teachers realize that they don't have to "wait for Superman" because *Superman is us*!

There is more. Consider South Simcoe Public School, in Durham District School Board, just east of Toronto. (The following account is taken from Dean, in press.) I take up this case because it shows more fully the role of parents, community, partnerships with the outside, student lives, and teacher struggles and successes.

Sandra Dean was raised in Trinidad with some strong communal values. As a teacher and budding administrator in Durham, she yearned for her first principalship, and in 1991 she received her first assignment. Her enthusiasm was immediately quieted when she found out it was Simcoe. The school was literally on the wrong side of the tracks. It was in the poorest community in all of Durham—a principal's nightmare, Sandra called it—located directly across from a strip mall. It was in an old rundown building in a community rife with economic and social problems— family disintegration, high unemployment, spousal and child abuse, drug and alcohol abuse, and more. Of the 89 schools in Durham, Simcoe was dead last in reading, writing, and math.

Like most principals in such situations (both Ryan and Jill did the same), Sandra started by sprucing up the building, drawing on her own family for painting, wallpapering, and putting up curtains during the summer before the school year started. In interaction with staff and students (although they would only believe it later when they experienced it), Sandra established a guiding principle: *Everyone has the right to be respected and the responsibility to respect others.* Remember Killer Slide No. 1, and its "impressive empathy"? In all negative cultures there is a strong ethos of disrespect. To begin to turn this around, leaders need to start respecting people before they have earned it. There is no other way to break the cycle and to go through the initial struggle of respecting others when they are not used to respecting anybody else, including you. Sandra Dean experienced this firsthand when the school opened. After she had put enormous effort into making the building more presentable, one of the first reactions from a teacher was "You seem to think that moving around classrooms and furniture, and adding a fresh coat of paint here and there is going to solve our problems. Well, it is not. Do you realize the kinds of things we have to deal with here?" Resolute moral purpose meets its first discouraging test!

Sandra persisted—new furniture, sports equipment, lights for the field, tackling the vandalism problem on the school's exterior by involving students. Over time, broken bottles and graffiti lessened and respect for the building increased. With staff, students, and teachers, the school agreed on a new motto: *Together we light the way.*

Some good things happened. A parent strung balloons around the new basketball court as a symbol of appreciation.

Students became more empathic to the caretaker, Gail, when with Sandra's support she dumped out the contents of a vacuum cleaner in front of senior students in one classroom in the context of a discussion on mutual respect. (This eventually led to a suggestion from one student that they conduct a 15-minute cleanup session each day, which was endorsed by all students.)

There was a mixture of brickbats and successes during the first two years. The following account alternates a disaster with a success.

Desmond was an angry eighth-grade student who bullied other kids and was a constant thorn in teachers' sides. He became increasingly more hostile and aggressive and no amount of contact brought a response from parents until eventually Sandra suspended Desmond. The next morning Desmond's father came to the school, stormed into Sandra's office, slammed the door, and launched into an angry tirade. Banging the desk, cursing and shouting, he yelled, "I am here to deal with you this time, you bitch! I'm going to teach you a lesson you will never forget. I'm fed up with you. I'm sick of you picking on my boy, picking on my family, picking on me!" Calling the police, court orders later, Desmond's father continued to harass Sandra by putting letters of condemnation on parents' windshields, yelling abuse at her at the end of the day, lurking around. It was only when Desmond left the school at the end of Grade 8 that the abuse stopped.

On the larger front, Sandra instituted the practice of "sunshine calls" to parents that teachers made to tell parents how well their children were doing and what a pleasure they were to teach. After initial suspicion, parents began to appreciate the calls and spread the word. Sandra leveraged the success of the "sunshine calls" to gently but firmly suggest that parents attend first report cards.

Leonard arrived in the middle of the year in Grade 6 from another Canadian city. He obviously was a troubled boy, and after some digging, Sandra found out that his mother, a prostitute, had been murdered. He loved his mother dearly, and after being taunted by other boys in his home city, he was sent east and ended up at Simcoe. One day he invited two boys to his home and invited them to meet his mom. He pulled out a ceramic urn with his mother's ashes and said, "Say hello to my mom." When he insisted and got no response, he went and got a shotgun and told them to say hello to his mom or get out of his house. Shortly after, Leonard left to go back out west. There were other stories of kids that could not be reached.

Ted, who transferred to the school in eighth grade, liked to carry a knife. And there was Bobby, who had head lice, whose hair was ripped out by his mother. And Melanie, who was taken away from her alcoholic mother and put in a foster home, and who responded that she did not want to be helped by all these do-gooders: "All they do is take me away from my mother and make us both cry. They left my mother alone with that guy [who was living with her] and put me in a foster home with a bunch of crappy people who sat around and smoked and drank all day."

For every Leonard, Ted, Bobby, and Melanie, there were a growing number of other kids who succeeded like never before. Roger, a 12-year-old with troubled history, arrived at Simcoe late one spring. He had a history of being extremely disruptive at the other schools he had attended. He was attracted to the theme of "respect others as you want to be respected." He was fascinated by "the Respect Lunch" program where the principal and teachers and Chief of the Durham Regional Police Services would cook lunch for the kids. He said he would start by "being the most respectful person you have ever seen." It then turned out that a male boarder at Roger's house who acted as a father died. Roger disappeared for many days and then showed up on Respect Lunch day. Sandra told him that she was glad to see him. "You worked hard for this meal." Roger responded, "It wasn't just for the food. I wanted to eat lunch with everybody and be part of the group. To tell you the truth, I really wanted to see if the police would serve someone like me."

Fred, an eighth-grade student, came with the record of "an inability to interact with others in a socially acceptable manner." He proceeded to target younger girls, making offensive remarks, ridiculing them until they burst into tears. Among other things, Fred had a serious problem with personal hygiene. Without singling out Fred, his teacher and teaching assistant decided to incorporate hygiene into the health class. Fred, took to this class and it had a big positive impact on him over time. Not the three R's, says Sandra, but it led to improvements in academics. Fred was still intermittently problematic. One day Sandra saw Fred walking down the hall when he passed a windowed door with a large smudge on it. He stopped, pulled out a small tissue from his pocket, and began wiping away the spot. Fred later began helping the custodian, and polished the particular pane of glass every day. Sandra says, "Fred had tasted success and he liked it!"

And Brad, another troubled 12-year-old, became successful, with Sandra observing, "All he needed was a decent, regular diet; he needed to know we cared about him; and he needed behavioral boundaries" (Dean, in press).

Sandra also led the school into a large number of community partnerships and support from General Motors, which has a huge plant in Oshawa, to Kodak, the Regional Police, local dentists, pizza places, and more—to the point where

South Simcoe won first prize in the country from the Conference Board of Canada for its outstanding partnerships, with
26 vibrant community and business links.

After two years there was no doubt that the school had a
strong socioemotional foundation both within the school and
with parents and the broader community. But the test results
came out, and Simcoe was dead last again in reading, writing,
and math. This was a huge blow to the school, as they thought
they were doing all the right things to establish the conditions
for academic success. Sandra, as with all other schools in the
district, had been establishing an increasingly precise focus on
instruction. Specifically, she had now put in place a threefold
strategy: a success mapping and achievement system (which
tracked individual student progress linked to instructional
responses), partnerships with the community (which had
become a vibrant success), and inclusive leadership (cultivat-
ing it across all staff).

Yet none of this appeared to be making a difference on the
bottom line. Nonetheless, Sandra was convinced that they were
on the right track. Her response was to tackle the achievement
problem head-on by strengthening the academic focus and
establishing a closer monitoring system with parents and teachers. One can easily surmise that the trusted, strong relationships that had been built over two years enabled them to move
more quickly and more deeply. And move they did. Three years
later, when the provincial tests were announced, 94% of South
Simcoe students were performing at the top two levels in reading, writing, and math. They were the highest-performing
inner-city school in the province.

The point about Crosby, Armadale, Rideau, and South
Simcoe is how they went from bad to great. They were not all
that motivated when they were bad, and in fact did not know
how to get out of the rut and probably did not think it was
possible. What changed their minds was not moral goading or

encouragement, and not research data that showed it was being done elsewhere in circumstances just like theirs. Rather, what made the difference was focused leadership that combined moral imperative and the pathways to get there. And this was based on the confidence of resolute leaders that once the right things kicked in, progress would generate its own new momentum.

One other key point here, which will become evident in the next chapter, is that the success we just witnessed is infinitely more likely and more sustainable when the district and all of its schools are jointly working on this agenda, which was the case for these four schools. The infrastructure, purposely built to enact the moral imperative, matters a great deal. It is no accident that Cassandra Costa and the teacher cited by Mary Jean Gallagher experienced brand-new success for themselves of the kind that they did not think possible. Changes in the *system at large* enabled it.

In short, *realized moral purpose* is the real moral imperative because it is the energizer that fuels and refuels the mission. "Good intentions" never was a viable strategy. Neiman (2009) makes the interesting point that the opposite of good is not bad, but good intentions. Very, very few educators have bad intentions, yet many are not successful in raising the bar and closing the gap. The moral imperative in my view, then, is not a matter of having good moral intentions, but rather being effective at realizing them. It ain't moral if it ain't working. Or as one of Curtis Linton's (2011) principals put it, "It's only equity if they actually do it."

CHICAGO: 100 SCHOOLS

In Chapter 1, we saw some Chicago schools courtesy of the careful research of Tony Bryk and his colleagues over the years. Their latest effort, *Organizing Schools for Improvement* (Bryk, Sebring, Allensworth, Luppescu, & Easton, 2010), sheds even more light on what success looks like and how to get there. Bryk et al. have well-documented longitudinal data from 1990 to the present on numerous measures of school quality and their impact on student achievement. There are some 480 elementary schools in the Chicago Public Schools system. Bryk et al. selected a sample of 118 of the most improving schools (in literacy and math) over the years and a parallel example of 118 stagnant or declining schools. They wanted to find out what made the difference in those schools that moved forward in the face of the same obstacles confronting those that languished.

The short and powerful answer is that one "driver" and four related factors caused success. The driver was school leadership—principals who acted like Ryan Friedman, Jill Maar, and Sandra Dean. These principals focused their work in four areas that they interconnected: links to parents and community, developing the professional capacities of teachers, deep instructional focus and coherence, and establishing a safe and secure environment for students that pressed and supported students to engage in "more ambitious intellectual activity" (Bryk et al., 2010, p. 65).

Schools that evidenced these qualities were 10 times more likely to be successful in engaging students and improving their performance in reading and math. Not a single school improved in either reading or math when weak academic supports for students "co-occurred with accounts from teachers attesting to weak social relations among the faculty and with parents" (Bryk et al., 2010, p. 123). No school improved that was weak on all five measures, and very few schools with strengths in the five domains failed to improve. And so on.

Most important for our purposes, these successes are not a matter of merely aligning five factors. Schools with strong instructional focuses were no better off unless they dynamically integrated the five elements. Curriculum and instructional coherence, say Bryk et al. (2010), is "a *social* activity as well as a technical act. Its development entails sustained work among teachers within and across grades" (p. 117, italics added).

It is crucial to grasp the persistence and depth of this work. Bryk et al. (2010) profile two schools within the sample, Hancock and Alexander Elementary Schools. These two schools started off in very similar ways, with strong emphasis on developing instructional capacity in reading. Less than two miles apart and serving similar neighborhoods, the two schools were dramatically different four years later. Hancock went from one of the 100 worst schools in Chicago to high performing. Alexander, by contrast, lost momentum to become fragmented, "suffering from both poor coordination and a lack of follow through" (p. 40) to become mired in a sense of hopelessness.

Once again we come to the *what* and the *how*. Hancock had a strong leader, Bonnie Whitmore, focusing on the right combination of factors (four domains, to be exact: parents and community, professional capacity, instructional depth and coherence, and student safety and press). She created a collective capacity and shared commitment that, as results began to accrue, generated more energy to build on initial success. Bonnie "combined an inclusive and facilitative approach to leadership, with a sustained, strategic focus on instructional improvement" (Bryk et al., 2010, p. 136).

The *how* is harder to get at because it requires the skill and touch of a gardener or a master chef. You have to have the right ingredients, but how to combine them dynamically is where the sophistication is. But as we set out to demonstrate in motion leadership, it is not a mystery. It requires continuous practice under conditions of feedback, support, and high expectations (Fullan, 2010a, 2010b).

The *how* is found in the blend of moral resoluteness, impressive empathy, and helping people realize moral purpose. According to Bryk et al. (2010), "principals establish both respect and personal regard when they acknowledge the vulnerabilities of others, actively listen to their concerns, and eschew arbitrary actions [and] couple this empathy with a compelling school vision" (p. 207), which they help enact. These *how* leaders are not afraid to be assertive. They are simultaneously directive, facilitative, and inclusive as they help create energized, effective communities. "Energy typically expended in resistance now gets redirected toward actually making one's ideas work" (p. 219)—a double moral victory.

I don't really need to provide more chapter and verse, but a brief reference to one more confirmatory set would help. Rick DuFour and his colleagues (DuFour, DuFour, Eaker, & Karhanek, 2010) have been deeply into the moral imperative and indeed this is reflected in the title their book, *Raising the Bar and Closing the Gap: Whatever It Takes.* In the six chapters reporting on specific named schools that are getting and having sustained success over many years, the same core focuses that we have been discussing show up time and again. Whether big or small, rural or urban, elementary, middle, or high schools, when determined moral imperative meets powerful core strategy, amazing things happen.

So far so good, but there is one problem. Realizing the moral imperative is a system proposition, not an individual school phenomenon. Put another way, Chicago should not have 118 schools out of 480 that are on the move. It should have 430 or more. Districtwide reform is the next moral frontier. Just like the film *Waiting for "Superman"* cannot solve the problem by showing the horrendous futility of the current system, and by calling for more passionate teachers and leaders, we cannot advance the moral imperative if we do not actually create the conditions for large swaths of the system to simultaneously pursue this agenda.

Thus, hidden in most of the stories in this chapter is a growing development of whole-system reform, or what I call *All Systems Go* (Fullan, 2010a). Nothing will happen on any scale until system leaders start taking their moral purpose seriously, living it day after day through strategic action. We actually now know quite a lot about how to do this. We start moving into the bigger system in the next chapter, with entire districts leveraging all of their schools forward.

CHAPTER THREE

School and District Symbiosis

Individual schools cannot get on—or if they do, cannot stay on—the moral track unless the whole district is working on the problem. District leadership is every bit as essential as school leadership—100% of the schools are implicated in this action. As before, we want to know exactly what this looks like in successful practice. In this chapter, I examine this through four districts: Sanger Unified School District, with 19 schools near Fresno, California; Fort Bend Independent School, with 75 schools near Houston, Texas; Ottawa Catholic District School Board, with 84 schools in Ontario, Canada; and York Region District School Board, with 192 schools in the greater Toronto area. All four of these districts and some of their schools were filmed as part of our motion leadership movie initiative (www.corwin-sinet.com/Michael_Fullan_Info.cfm). Three of the districts have also been written up as case examples (Sanger in DuFour, DuFour, Eaker, & Karhanek, 2010; Ottawa and York in Fullan, 2010a). Given the range of district size, from 19 to almost 200 schools, I can safely say that these examples, with their consistent themes, cover the vast majority of cases. In the moral imperative realized, all excuses come off the table.

SANGER UNIFIED SCHOOL DISTRICT

Sanger is a sprawling rural district in the valley just east of Fresno, where the population of the district has changed dramatically over the past decade. At present, 70% of its students are Hispanic, 18% white, and 10% Asian. More than 75% of the students qualify for free or reduced lunch. The majority of students are English language learners. In 2003–2004, Sanger was designated by the state of California as a Program Improvement district, which meant that it was a failing district—a district "in dire straits," said the superintendent, Marc Johnson.

In 2003–2004, the percentages of students at or above proficiency in math and language arts were 31% and 27%, respectively. By 2007–2008, the corresponding figures were 59% and 50%. This short and powerful journey is a story of the moral imperative in action districtwide.

In broad strokes and drawing from our motion leadership movie story, the flow of success went along the following lines. First, the Program Improvement designation was treated as a timely wake-up call. The district was preparing for action at the time, but the negative label created a greater sense of urgency.

Second, as in all cases of successful moral imperative, the superintendent began to establish a guiding coalition at the central level—a focused team that mirrored and reinforced the new direction. Because Sanger is small, the core team consisted of Superintendent Johnson; Deputy Superintendent

Rich Smith, who heads curriculum and instruction; and an associate superintendent of human resources.

Third, again similar to other examples, the district emphasized a small number of inspiring priorities and pursued them relentlessly. There were three in particular: hope is not a strategy, don't blame the kids, and it's about learning—simple, powerful, and memorable. Everyone in the system at all levels can tell you about the big three. Notice also that these priorities capture purpose and strategy.

Fourth, the district leadership began to make personnel changes, particularly at the school leadership level. It now became crystal clear that to be a principal in Sanger meant that you had to be a deep instructional leader.

Fifth, the district began to systematically invest in team-based capacity building, beginning with teams getting immersed in professional learning communities, taking advantage of regional professional development with the DuFours, and adding and integrating "response to intervention" and direct instruction. These three elements became closely integrated as the instructional core of the district's work.

Finally, Sanger established transparency and openness about practice and results. In what I have called *learning is the work* (Fullan, 2008), the district created means by which learning from each other and accountability became built into daily, weekly, and annual routines.

I will furnish more detail in a moment, but note that this list of six elements of the strategy is not mysterious. It captures what I call "the skinny of change"—the smallest number of key things that you have to do well and in concert (Fullan, 2010b, 2010c).

DuFour and his colleagues (2010) give us more detail. They identify five key elements: systems of intervention, developing principals as leaders, the very powerful annual Sanger Summits, administrative retreats, and ongoing support and focus.

With respect to systems of intervention, the superintendent "insisted that each school create a plan for providing additional time and support for students who experienced difficulty" (DuFour et al., 2010, p. 153). The district also helped schools develop the capacity to find and implement better instructional practices for diagnosing and helping individual students. With new leadership at the school level leading the process, all schools mobilized combinations of adults to intensify direct support for students. It was an "all hands on deck" proposition (p. 155).

The Sanger Summits represent a potent strategy of bringing problems and success out in the open. The sequence is crucial here. After receiving training and in an overall climate of nonjudgmentalism (it's okay to make mistakes as long as you learn; if results show problems, nothing negative will happen as long as you start working on the problem; etc.), principals are clearly on the line:

> Each fall, the Sanger Summit brings building principals and central office staff together for a structured review of student achievement. Principals from three schools at a time (grouped by similar characteristics) meet for a dialogue with Superintendent Johnson, the associate superintendent of human resources, and Deputy Superintendent Smith. The conversation takes place in full view of curriculum coordinators, program directors, guests from other districts, county office representatives, and staff and students of local universities who come to observe the process.
>
> Each principal provides a 45-minute overview of trends in student achievement in his or her school and the progress the school is making in implementing professional learning community concepts.
>
> Questions are posed, ideas for action are identified, and plans are made for further action by the principal. Johnson contends that "the constant transparency

of results and the collective approach to problem solving have caused the depth of knowledge of the district's
principals to grow exponentially." (DuFour et al., 2010,
pp. 155–156)

In addition to the summits, all leaders meet every August
at an annual retreat where goals and strategies are reviewed
and further specified. This degree of precision is key because
it clarifies exactly what works and why. Expectations for principals as leaders are also specifically reinforced.

Finally, ongoing support and focus is always on the agenda.
Every year, intensive training is provided for a new group of
district educators. Collaboration, and schools learning from
each other, is established by setting up small groups of schools
(three or four) whose representatives meet regularly and conduct cross-school learning visits in which, for example, teachers in single-grade schools get an opportunity to learn from
their counterparts in other schools.

In Sanger and in the other three districts that we will turn
to, the collective pride and allegiance—and intriguingly, the
sense of collaborative competition—flourishes. If you ask any
educator who was in the district prior to the change if they
would ever go back to the old way, the response is always an
enthusiastic and unanimous "never."

Quite simply, districts like Sanger, with all their challenges
and their obvious success, are a joy to work in. As Marc
Johnson observes, five years ago if you were to ask a teacher
in June how he or she was doing, the teacher would say, "I am
really exhausted and can't wait for the summer." Now he says
he never gets that reply. It is more like, "We worked hard and
need a break, but let me tell you what we are going to do next
year." At the point in May–June when energy should be at the
lowest, people are still pumped.

In other words, moral purpose realized is the best working condition a teacher will ever experience. In Sanger, state

achievement results have increased by 40 points. Scores on the state's Academic Achievement Index have increased in each and every school by at least 118 points, with an average increase of 198 points. In 2002, all Sanger schools ranked in the bottom half of the state. By 2007, all were in the top half, with 10 schools in the top decile. Several of the schools have won awards, including Blue Ribbon recognition, that are appreciated as district accomplishments.

Sanger is great, but it is not alone.

FORT BEND INDEPENDENT SCHOOL DISTRICT

Fort Bend Independent School District, in Sugar Land, Texas, is almost evenly diverse: 31% black, 24% Hispanic, 23% white, and 21% Asian. Of its 68,000 students in 75 schools, 43% are considered to be at risk. Tim Jenney became superintendent in 2005, having just come from a district in Virginia in which he introduced new approaches targeted at districtwide reform. He had success, but it seemed slow—six years to get good progress. (The ideas in this section came largely from Fullan, 2010c.)

As he thought about his new challenge, Tim saw two things. The history of site-based management at Fort Bend had created a system of individual schools, not a school system. And the geographical organization of area schools had resulted in individual fiefdoms. He knew that he needed focus, coherence, and corresponding systemwide commitment.

The story of Fort Bend is pretty much like Sanger's in its thematic strategies, but perhaps more assertive and demanding. There were very high expectations but also lots of support and careful judgment. Balancing, in fact integrating, support and accountability is a clever feature of system success. But the press was on for immediate success. I call the Fort Bend story The Velvet Hammer.

What took Tim Jenney six years in Virginia was accomplished in three years in Fort Bend. In that time, reading, math, and science increased by 7%. The number of "recognized" (80% of students achieving proficiency on the state tests) and "exemplary" (90% proficiency) schools in the state assessment system climbed from 9 in 2008 to 45 in 2009.

Fort Bend put the moral imperative on a high pedestal and married it with an aggressive capacity-building strategy that integrated focus and accountability. In particular, the district mobilized leadership to this end. Working simultaneously at the district and school levels, the district established a new guiding coalition away from area superintendencies toward a tightly knit team of central leaders. With a central team of about eight people—some of whom had direct-line responsibility with principals and others provided strong support in data management and accountability, and human resources— the district formed a two-way partnership with schools and fostered school-to-school learning and mutual identity.

As in all cases, the district dramatically signaled that principals were to be dedicated instructional leaders. About 50% of principals turned over in the three-year period; over 70% had left or retired by the fifth year. Teacher leadership was also part and parcel of the new focus, with "campus coordinators" positioned as school improvement officers who worked with principals and the district on the same core agenda.

The combination of concentrated leaders focused—again, as we have seen in every case so far—on common assessment frameworks linked to individualized instructional practices. Progress and problems were also transparent. The district engaged in monitoring and solving problems using its equivalent of the Sanger Summits; that is, results on annual achievement became transparent to all, with corresponding discussion of how to improve results.

There is palpable pride and knowledge across all schools about how and why the district has been successful. There seems to be equal measures of relentless pressure to do better and a relaxed confidence among teachers and administrators about district success. Attending to every focused detail that is necessary for success is built into the district's culture. There is no way that the moral imperative could be neglected either as a fervent goal or in relation to the strategy to continuously realize it. This is a district that demonstrates the speed of quality implementation. It clearly proves that successful whole-system reform in a large, challenging, diverse district can be achieved in an impressively short time period. It also demonstrates that this is a forever proposition. There are always new students, new staff, new leaders to be cultivated and never-ending attention to be paid to reducing the gap and to going deeper into learning skills and competencies.

In all these district cases, the stories of purpose and strategy are remarkably similar, even though most of the leaders have never met each other.

OTTAWA CATHOLIC DISTRICT SCHOOL BOARD

Jamie McCracken, the director (chief superintendent) of Ottawa Catholic District since 2003, was a high school principal in the district prior to his promotion and worked briefly in the district office. He describes the culture back then with one word: *clenched*. The director at the time issued 13 thrusts annually that were supposed to be the themes for the year. Each year there were a different 13. Jamie learned that he never had to "thrust back," as there was no follow-through. He ran a good school but he knew that he was totally detached from the district and his colleagues. He was promoted to change that.

Jamie and his coleaders have used virtually every major theme that I have covered in this book. And they did it without any direct outside help other than drawing on good ideas and taking advantage of new resources.

The Ottawa Catholic District School Board is one of 29 Catholic districts in Ontario's public education system (which has a total of 72; Catholic districts are fully publicly funded per the Canadian constitution established at the time of federation). The district has approximately 42,000 students in 84 schools. The demographics in the catchment area of Canada's capital city range from affluent to disadvantaged, including large numbers of immigrants who arrive without English language skills.

Jamie started as superintendent with some large-scale meetings that he called Re-imagining Days. For the first time in the history of the system, he included nonprofessionals—support staff, custodians, technicians, and bus drivers. Knowing something about emphasis on a small number of goals and staying the course, he selected three core priorities: student success (e.g., ensure high levels of critical literacy), success for staff (e.g., build collaborative learning communities through shared leadership), and stewardship of resources (e.g., align human and operational resources to support and close gaps in student achievement). These have been the same three priorities every year for the past seven years.

The system glue—the same kind we saw in Sanger and Fort Bend—is fostered in three interrelated ways: constant communication with all groups, precision-based capacity-building and problem-solving strategies, and a careful pursuit of personnel policies and recruitment of leaders who are selected and developed to serve the three core goals.

Jamie has built in two-way communication sessions with all groups—principals, teachers, support staff, parents, community members, and union leaders. He sees all 4,000 employees as his constituency. He knows about one of the "skinny rules": Communication during implementation is far more important than communication prior to implementation (Fullan, 2010b). Keep the message simple, keep it focused and consistent, keep conveying it, and talk about the results, the problems, and the strategies as you go.

With respect to the second means of focusing—precision-based intervention—a host of interrelated strategies are under way. The central district structure and personnel were reorganized to overcome previous silos so that leadership could operate as a guiding coalition, again with the same message and emphasis on the district's three basic goals. Jamie introduced a critical literacy framework requiring schools to focus on literacy by building their individual and collective capacity. This was not invitational; it was presented as nonnegotiable. The system provided all kinds of support in terms of resources, coaches, data access, SMART Goals (those that are Specific, Measurable, Attainable, Realistic, and Timely), time for job-embedded learning, and the like. There was an atmosphere of risk taking and learning, as long as you were focused on solving problems with respect to the core priorities.

The work got more and more specific, another characteristic of successful systems: precision increases. The buddy system (in which teachers and students in Grades 1–3 are "buddied" with their counterparts in Grades 4–6 for one day a month) is used by most schools. Teachers co-plan and co-teach; relationships get built as teachers, students, and school leaders become more and more precise about instruction.

The system has become more and more focused. For example, the district discovered that the 10 largest elementary schools were, for the most part, doing "good" but not "great." They were getting respectable results in the low 70% range, but Jamie challenged them to do better. He and others helped the principals examine their instructional practice with a view to moving toward a more focused approach involving personalization, precision, and professional learning. Jamie shared the C. D. Howe report (Johnson, 2009) with them, which compared school results in the province by comparing like districts with like districts. The report stated that because of the demographics of Ottawa's suburban population, these principals should be getting much higher results in their schools. With help from the district leadership, these schools responded by increasing expectations, changing teaching practices, and getting better results.

Similarly, in September 2007 the district started the Engagement Project, which targets students showing signs of decreased school engagement. Based on indicators of student tracking and achievement results, six schools in the district were selected to participate. Four youth workers were appointed to the position of engagement coach, whose role is to personally engage with the students regularly, assist with behavioral interventions, help with learning strategies, make home visits when necessary, participate in team meetings to review cases, and liaise and collaborate with community agencies. The results from the evaluation of the project show a decline in absences, lateness, and suspensions. Key intervention strategies that worked included providing students with alternative learning experiences, individualizing programs for students, and monitoring and maintaining regular contact with students.

Another powerful intervention has been the Senior Kindergarten Tutoring Program, which identifies five-year-olds who are seriously behind in oral language and literacy skills. The program runs from September to June and consists of an extra half-day of learning five days a week over and above the regular kindergarten program. Four qualified teachers, appointed to the position of tutor, implemented a variety of programming activities and learning experiences that were all viewed through the lens of oral language. The results from the program, which uses a quasi-experimental design, show that the program was successful for all students, both male and female, and was especially beneficial for English language learners. By spring, the students in the tutoring program out-performed or performed similarly to the comparison group on most of the assessments. Further, these students were already beginning to show transfer of emergent literacy skills to read a text, with some students attaining the district read-ing targets for Grade 1 before the end of the first term.

All this work on instruction is buttressed with basic, always focused professional learning communities within schools and the use of networks of schools, such as the math network in which several schools are learning from each other and linking better instruction to better results.

There is one more major reinforcer of cohesion: the deliberate use of personnel policies and leadership recruitment and devel-opment. Jamie has been blunt with vice principals, telling them that if they want to get promoted in this system, they have to be curriculum and instruction leaders. He started to identify future leaders by "tapping them on the shoulder" and getting them into future leaders programs. The district always has a list of 15–20 names of teacher leaders, vice principals, and principals who would make strong instructional leaders. There are also leader-ship programs for support staff and maintenance staff.

Everyone in the system, including custodians, knows what the three key goals are and how the system is doing relative to results. And how are they doing? From 2005 to 2009, all six scores (Grades 3 and 6 reading, writing, and math) have improved from a baseline of about 60%, on the average, to 66% (Grade 3 reading), 75% (Grade 3 writing), 76% (Grade 3 math), 74% (Grade 6 reading), 74% (Grade 6 writing), and 69% (Grade 6 math).

High school achievement is equally impressive. Grade 10 literacy results are 89%, well above the provincial average. When results came out in August 2009, showing 2%–9% increases over 2008, Jamie displayed the data on a slide at a meeting with all school principals. As the cheers rose, the superintendents entered the room carrying trays of champagne to celebrate the accomplishments. This district is not finished and is well on its way to eliminating the achievement gap between socioeconomic groups.

The leadership at Ottawa Catholic at both the district and school levels is preoccupied with improving student achievement. It is almost all they talk about—strategies, what results are we getting, and what specifically more can we do. It is about the whole child.

As director, Jamie inherited the running of a Social Justice Fund. Its three priorities were facilities, technology, and poverty. Guess what? It never got around to poverty (too amorphous or daunting?), and its $60,000 base more or less stayed as is. Jamie changed that. He eliminated the first two priorities and invited all employees in the system to donate to the fund. It works this way: Any principal can put in a request for a small-scale poverty-related item (e.g., food, clothes, epi-pen), and Jamie commits to responding with the money within 24 hours. That fund is now steady at $350,000 per year and is spent down every year.

All of this development and success at Ottawa Catholic is occurring because the district has mastered the small number of key things that make all systems go. It combines a moral imperative, a relentless focus (always on message), precision, high-yield instructional strategies, focus on data and results, and the cultivation of leadership at all levels to engage everyone in the moral purpose of improvement for all.

YORK REGION DISTRICT SCHOOL BOARD

York Region District School Board (YRDSB) is a large, multicultural urban district that is part of the greater Toronto area and has 130,000 students, 8,800 teachers, and 192 schools. In 1989, the new director (superintendent), Bill Hogarth, stunned the system when he said that all YRDSB students should be reading at the end of Grade 1. There started a 10-year journey of capacity building and, deeper still, sustainable realization, which Lyn Sharratt, the recently retired superintendent of curriculum and instruction, and I recently wrote about (Sharratt & Fullan, 2009). Bill put together a leadership team that never strayed off message as they built collective capacity.

Once again we have a combination of strategies that excited people about moral purpose, focused capacity building, and above all developed a strong sense of partnership between the district and the schools, across schools, and between schools and the community. Without strong two-way partnerships and targeted individual and collective capacity building, moral purpose would only be a slogan.

The core of capacity building was 13 parameters that the schools and the district developed together (see Exhibit 3.1).

Exhibit 3.1 Thirteen Parameters From *Realization*

1. Shared beliefs and understanding

2. Embedded literacy coaches

3. Time-tabled literacy block

4. Principal leadership

5. Early and ongoing intervention

6. Case management approach

7. Literacy professional development at school staff meetings

8. In-school grade/subject meetings

9. Book rooms with leveled books and resources

10. Allocation of budget for literacy resources

11. Action research focused on literacy

12. Parental involvement

13. Cross-curricular literacy connections

Source: Sharratt & Fullan, 2009.

There is no need to discuss the 13 parameters in detail except to say that school teams and district staff work together (through professional learning sessions and day-to-day work) to implement the parameters in all schools and classrooms. I talked about the sine qua non importance of *collective* capacity building, that is, the team, the group, the organization, and the system working together to get better. A visitor can go into any one of the 192 schools in YRDSB and have similar conversations—the language of focused instruction is ubiquitous. A principal or vice principal can move to a new school and find a critical mass of kindred spirits. It is noteworthy that we have recently added a fourteenth "wraparound" parameter, "shared responsibility and accountability," which is internalized self and group commitment to the moral imperative and how to accomplish it.

YRDSB deliberately builds whole-system, all-schools reform, working continually on what I would call the *social glue* of capacity building—the collegiality and instructional practices that enable everyone in the district to pull together. Good practice produces commitment. Committed people pursue even better practices. And the scaffolding to do all this operates at three permeable levels—district, networked schools, and schools.

At the district level the Literacy Collaborative contains the overall framework of shared vision and related capacity building involving the 13 parameters. Professional learning sessions with leadership teams from all schools take place several times a year (schools are in one of four cohorts because of the large numbers). The same message and two-way communication about purpose and progress occurs throughout. An annual Literacy Fair—in which all 192 schools in the district prepare and share 25-minute multimedia accounts of what they set out to do for the year and what they accomplished—reinforces the substance of what the schools are doing and strengthens the collective identity and commitment to the overall endeavor.

The next level is more operational. Every school belongs to a geographically organized Learning Network (LN) consisting of 6–10 schools in a cluster. There are 22 LNs, and they focus on specific practices, student results, cross-school sharing, learning to do better, and mutual commitment. They engage in collaborative competition with each other and with the rest of the district. When they do meet, participants consist of school principals and leadership teams; the superintendent, who is the coordinator of the LN; and district curriculum consultants. If you observe an LN session, you will see that no one dominates. They are colearners, with practice and results as the drivers. It is noteworthy that Bill Hogarth delayed the establishment of the LNs for seven months despite strong pleas from his area superintendents because he wanted to make sure that whole-district commitment was in place, thereby trying to avoid LNs becoming isolated fiefdoms. Effective leaders always have an eye on allegiance to the system as a whole while they also support smaller-scale intensive learning partnerships.

The third level is the school which we have already seen in detail in the cases of Crosby Heights and Armadale. These schools are especially successful because they are part and parcel of a larger infrastructure that works on systemwide moral imperative.

The overall effect is that ideas, leadership, and commitment flow readily across the system. YRDSB has a high-trust, transparent learning culture in which mistakes are treated as part of growth, and moral purpose (*all* kids can learn) is taken seriously by all as job one.

It works. Despite being one of the largest, most diverse districts in Ontario, YRDSB is one of the best. It has raised achievement scores across the provincial measures of reading, writing, and math for Grades 3 and 6 by some 15% over the past five years, along with increasing its Grade 10 literacy scores and its high school graduation rates. And when progress seemed to plateau a couple of years ago, the district stayed and deepened the course. In 2009 when the scores again jumped up, the excitement around the district was palpable. It seems that the struggle itself makes gains all the more satisfying.

DISTRICT AND SCHOOL SYMBIOSIS

These four districts cover the range from small to medium to large districts. Yet the stories are remarkably similar in focus and in strategy. It takes leadership that focuses on a small number of goals and corresponding powerful strategies that they employ in concert. These leaders didn't go to management books or research to discover what had to be done. Rather, they started with practice, learned from their experience, and learned from others (Fullan, in press).

There are two big forces for change that I have identified in this work. One concerns mutual allegiance and the other collaborative competition. When educators work as partners, both vertically between schools and the central district and with peers across schools, they naturally develop a strong sense of mutual identity. One way of expressing this is that school principals become almost as concerned about the success of other schools as they do about their own school. Everyone starts to identify with the success of the system. Everyone takes pride in whole-system accomplishments and reaches out to help each other whenever it is called for. And everyone works easily together within and across schools.

The second powerful phenomenon is not one that anyone planned for or expected. I have come to call it *collaborative competition*. Because the stakes are so high—the moral imperative for all—and because progress is so crucial and so out in the open for all to see, people start to compete with themselves (we can do better than last year) and with each other (we can do better than them). But it is competition within the family. It is not win/lose but wins leveraging wins. It is a kind of Moral Olympics where people compete for the greater good and get great satisfaction from the struggle and the results. You don't have to plan for collaborative competition; just create the conditions we have seen in these four districts and then appreciate the windfall.

What we are seeing with the moral imperative coupled with focused, specific strategies is increasingly larger proportions of the system acting as system leaders. Ultimately, addressing the moral imperative depends on the deliberate cultivation of habits of system leadership among all leaders, regardless of what level of the system they work from.

The development of scores of leaders with system awareness and investment is the cure to the fundamental problems uncovered in the film *Waiting for "Superman."* Leaders who mobilize collective capacity that drives, as much as it is driven by, the moral imperative is what gets results on a large scale. Leadership finds its multiple niches.

CHAPTER FOUR

System Leaders

O nce moral imperative gets on the move, becomes more visible, and gets linked to action, it inevitably pulls you outward and upward. I call it *system leadership*, and it takes three forms. One concerns school leaders who become more committed to linking to other schools while still staying in their own principalship. A second involves school leaders who take positions that oversee or otherwise help other schools. The third is system leaders themselves who undertake direct whole-system reform. By *system*, I mean all of the schools in a district, state/province, or country.

SCHOOL LEADERS BROADEN THEIR PERSPECTIVE

We saw in the last chapter the allegiance that is generated when districts help schools work together as peers in relation to each other's agenda within a district framework. I need not repeat the details here except to say that the principal's role is once again shifting. It has changed in the past seven years to be unequivocally focused on instructional leadership. Now we see an extension of this phenomenon. The new role

57

definition of the principal includes the requirement that he or she has the explicit responsibility to learn from other schools as well as to contribute to their betterment. Each of the four districts featured in the previous chapters is a prime example of this evolution. The principals within these districts are expected to be, and see themselves as, responsible for not only their school but also the progress of other schools and the district as a whole. This is their new moral imperative, and the entire system benefits.

The value of these directions is emphatically confirmed in the new Wallace Foundation study of the impact of leadership on student learning (Seashore Louis, Leithwood, Wahlstrom, & Anderson, 2010). Among the main findings are that (1) collective leadership (when the group is mobilized) is far more impactful than individual leadership, (2) principals' impact on student learning is indirect (but nonetheless specific) through improving the working conditions (resources, focus, data, monitoring, etc.) of teachers, and (3) in high-performing schools everyone's sense of influence and moral purpose is enhanced. The moral pie gets bigger. People collaborate within the school, and they seek outside connections to help them (and those on the outside) go further.

When this outward-facing habit gets ingrained, additional powerful things can happen. One interesting example concerns Illinois's District 96, a small district of 11 schools. The superintendent, Tom Many, and his colleagues have used professional learning community strategies to change the culture of the district in order to become a strong learning system, with measurable benefits for all (DuFour, DuFour, Eaker, & Karhanek, 2010).

I could have easily and correctly included District 96 in the previous chapter as another example of districtwide success. However, I want to introduce it here for another reason. Because it is a small district, there are only so many internal resources to draw on, and after a while people begin to want additional connections. After hearing me present at a national conference on the power of *lateral capacity building,* in which peers learn from each other, Tom came up with a great idea. He proposed to his principals that they each link up with a sister school in other districts in the region. Some principals were skeptical that it would prove worth the effort, but they were willing to try. I asked Tom to send me an account of how the idea turned out, and this is what he wrote:

The sister school exchange began with a small pilot three years ago and has grown a bit larger each year. We are tapping into lateral capacity through the lens of Professional Learning Communities, and reinforcing the learning with an end-of-the-year learning fair. The results of this project have been very powerful.

Planning and participating in a sister school exchange is now a required professional development activity for each building principal and has been incorporated into their school improvement planning effort. We created a brief application form that each principal completes and submits for review. The application form is not intended to be an accountability measure but is more in the spirit of Elmore's concept of Reciprocal Accountability. As the superintendent of schools, I want to know what they are working on so I can support their efforts to improve.

Each principal is required to identify a sister school that has a reputation for expertise in a specific area related to the principal's school improvement plan. The expectation is that the area of excellence or expertise that the sister school possesses is connected and associated with the principal's school improvement goals for that year. In its simplest form, principals are asked to reach out through their networks and find a school that has demonstrated they are successfully dealing with an area of need for the principal's own school.

Once the sister school is identified, the District 96 principal makes contact and establishes a relationship. As part of that initial conversation, the District 96 principal describes the rationale for why this partnership makes sense and why it will be beneficial to all concerned. We still approach the sister school exchange through the lens of Professional Learning Communities because we want to continuously reinforce the concepts and drive the Big Ideas deeper into our culture, but it is the teachers and principals who are changing the conversation from the "what" to a discussion of the "how" and "why" as they learn from one another. I think you would love to watch them "making meaning" of their work. It is clear that the practitioner-to-practitioner connection has been a powerful way for our teachers to learn.

The logistics for the visit are established after the sister school has been identified. Dates and times are scheduled, and team members are identified. The actual visit itself takes place in one day where the visiting school asks questions based upon the probe they have developed for the receiving school. The receiving school answers their questions, produces artifacts, shares insights, and so on. The logistics are the easy stuff, but it is also where many of our principals got stuck because once the details of the visit are in place, each principal is charged with the responsibility of creating a "probe" to guide the visit.

Initially, the probes were broadly written around very general Professional Learning Community concepts such as providing evidence of the presence of a guaranteed and viable curriculum, or a balanced and coherent system of assessment, or systematic pyramids of intervention. More recently, principals have begun to narrow the scope by seeking more detailed and in-depth information about the successful implementation of specific concepts related to his or her school improvement plan. We are quickly moving from a superficial "what" conversation to a more important "how" and "why" conversation.

We have discovered that the learning is two-way. Obviously, we learn a lot from the schools we visit, the program we observe, and the teachers with whom we talk. The best way for people to change is to do it themselves, and to learn from others similarly engaged. To see other people who are a lot like them being successful with the change is powerful and specific. Watching other people who are a lot like you generates so many positive results. We found that if the principal targets his or her sister school visit carefully, the visit can do more to help his or her teachers learn and grow than any "sit and get" inservice program.

We have found the reverse is also true as well. We learn from others when we visit their school, but when the sister schools come to visit District 96, our teachers learn as they prepare to present information about our practices to the other school. Anytime our teachers have to prepare and present, they report that they learn at a deeper level. Teachers report that the process of preparing to speak to visitors is very powerful in terms of sustaining our practices and driving them deeper into our culture.

Another component of our efforts to build lateral capacity may be the annual Chautauqua we hold. In the spirit of continuous improvement, teams of teacher leaders and principals gather for a one-day planning event at the end of each school year. The focus of the Chautauqua is on reconciling the various views regarding what was accomplished during the previous school year.

Teams of teachers and administrators review individual school and District SMART Goals, revisit the current reality of our progress toward completion of long-range goals, and develop recommendations for the tasks, initiatives, and goals that will be considered for the upcoming school year. The Chautauqua concludes with a "learning fair" where each school reports on an important aspect of their work during the past year. Last year, the pilot schools reported on their sister school visits. This year each school will be reporting on their sister school visits.

I have not heard a single negative comment about the sister school exchange idea, and in most cases the teachers who have participated are not only positive but rave about what they learned and how successful the experience was in helping them see other ways to improve their teaching and learning. If this is lateral capacity, then we need more of it!

I also like the fact that the sister school strategy builds on a "positive deviant" approach. We go out seeking other schools that have demonstrated unusual success with a particular aspect of teaching and learning we want to know more about. The fact that we go and learn from others, and they from us, creates a kind of celebratory feeling around the process of learning from one another. (Tom Many, personal communication, July 2009)

There is nothing profound about this example. It merely takes the concept of action-oriented moral imperative and extends it into a purposeful, focused learning initiative with a wider but manageable network of schools. It is consistent with what we learned in the last chapter and merely fleshes it out in an innovative manner. It represents a new way of working for incumbent school principals in which they remain as principals but widen the moral net, whether with schools within their districts or beyond.

SCHOOL LEADERS AS FORMAL SYSTEM LEADERS

The National College for Leadership of Schools and Children's Services (NC) in England formally adopted "school heads as system leaders" as one of its main themes. The NC is responsible for developing and supporting school heads and leaders of children's services throughout England. This is the organization's definition of system leadership:

> Leaders working within and beyond their individual organizations; sharing and harnessing the best resources that the system can offer to bring about improvement in their own and other organizations; and influencing thinking, policy, and practice so as to have a positive impact on the lives and life chances of all children and young people. (For more information on the National College, see www.nationalcollege.org.uk/index/about-us/national-college-membership.htm.)

There are several elements to the program. One involves the selection and identification of outstanding school principals to the formal status of National Leader of Education. These leaders are publicly acknowledged and are available on a short- or long-term basis to help schools "in special measures" (the English designation for failing schools). They also are invited to give input on national policy matters and are consulted on other educational issues.

A similar designation identifies schools that have great track records of improvement and, after screening, are identified as National Support Schools (NSSs). In the latter case, the school head and the whole school staff are engaged by struggling schools via a contractual arrangement to help them improve.

Another cluster involves federations, trusts, and academies that work as partners and clusters to improve each other. We recently filmed a primary school federation in England as part of our Motion Leadership movie. The St John/St James federation in Hackney, a borough in inner London, started after one school (St John/St James is a single school) with great school leadership went from special measures to outstanding. When the district contemplated what to do with a second school that was in special measures, it was decided that St John/St James should partner with that school, with the St John/St James school head becoming "executive head" of both schools. The turnaround was so successful that a third and fourth school have been added to the cluster. There is one executive head that runs the cluster, with each of the other three schools having principals who report to her. Teachers and leaders across the schools learn from each other, leaders are moved where they are needed, and leadership mentoring and development are built in.

One doesn't have to follow this English model literally (for more information on these various arrangements and programs, see www.nationalcollege.org.uk). Any strategy that partners schools and gives people leadership responsibility across the schools is compatible with these principles of system leadership.

Ontario, Canada, has a program similar to the NSS strategy, although not so formal in status, called Schools on the Move. Some 140 schools are identified as having made substantial progress in literacy or numeracy over a three-year period. They are profiled on demographics, strategies, and results, which are reported in two pages on the Literacy Numeracy Secretariat's website (www.edu.gov.on.ca/eng/literacynumeracy/publications.html). Money is made available for other schools to learn from them. Both sets of schools learn. The moral imperative and sense of responsibility to other schools and to the system as a whole are palpable. The point is that school principals, when the system enables it and when it is done in a spirit of partnership (i.e., nonpunitive), take easily and naturally to this wider system leadership responsibility.

Make no mistake about it: The work of the National College in England and the Ontario Literacy/Numeracy Secretariat in Ontario is precisely driven by moral purpose in action. According to the NC, system leadership is all about

- being driven by a moral purpose,
- improving all children and young people's lives regardless of which school or children's center they attend or neighborhood in which they live,
- recognizing the reciprocal benefits derived from peer-to-peer support,
- ensuring there is a positive impact with measurable outcomes,
- accepting collective responsibility and shared accountability for the performance of the system, and
- increasingly moving from intervention to prevention.

This strong trend of outstanding school leaders taking responsibility beyond their own schools is powerful and is bound to expand. Incidentally, the same argument can and should be made about superintendents, namely, that strong district leaders such as the four we saw in Chapter 3 should be running two or more districts. This applies especially to the United States, where many states have 800 or more tiny districts operating in a terribly inefficient, and in many cases ineffective, manner. It would be a step forward if we began to see "executive superintendents" running two or more small districts.

SYSTEM LEADERS THEMSELVES

The moral imperative in action at the whole-system level is becoming increasingly crucial and, thankfully, receiving much more attention by system leaders. Here we are talking about entire states, provinces, and countries. A large part of their job, of course, is to foster leadership at other levels of the system, such as those we examined in the previous three chapters. They have to develop the policies and strategies, and create the conditions under which the moral imperative does actually become realized. This is demanding work; they have to get their own state house in order and then engage the sector in multiple two-way partnerships. But they have dug a hole for themselves in the past decade, where the moral imperative is pervasive, but only in rhetoric. It is not necessarily that central leaders' intentions have been suspect, but as I have said time and time again, moral imperative is not a strategy.

Lately, we in Ontario and others around the world have been engaged in making it happen. This work was vividly displayed at Building Blocks for Education, an international conference in September 2010 that was hosted by the premier of Ontario and cochaired by Sir Michael Barber and me. Detailed presentations were made on successful examples of whole-system reform (from Finland, Ontario, and Singapore) and on two systems just embarking on explicit system reform (Australia and the United States). Another presentation was made by Andreas Schleicher, head of the Analysis and Indicator Division of the Program for International Student Assessment, who is examining what makes certain countries successful in raising the bar and closing the gap in student achievement. In short, there is rapidly growing interest in making whole-system reform happen. And the more you make it happen, the more energizing it becomes for all—the more it takes on accelerating momentum.

To take Ontario as an example, it is not so much that we invented the ideas but rather that we have had the opportunity to put them into practice comprehensively since 2003, when a new government was elected. The premier, Dalton McGuinty, was deeply committed to the moral imperative of raising the bar and closing the gap for all children, and he was equally committed to implementing a focused strategy to get there. At the starting point in 2003, Ontario's public school system was stagnant. Its two million students and 4,900 schools in 72 districts had been stuck or had flatlined in literacy, numeracy, and high school graduation for the previous five years. Six years later, literacy had moved upward by 14%, and high school graduation rates climbed from 68% to 79%. What happened is a story essentially similar to what we saw in Chapter 3, but on a whole-system basis. Let's start with the moral purpose of the leader.

Dalton McGuinty, premier of Ontario, is just finishing his seventh year in office. From day one, he was not only committed to making whole-system improvements but equally concerned about how to get there. At the Building Blocks for Education summit, McGuinty delivered a speech in which he cited eight lessons that come from his immersion in whole-system reform (see Exhibit 4.1).

This is resolute leadership. It is about purpose and action. In Lesson 1, McGuinty (2010) says that "teachers and principals can smell a fad a thousand miles away," and thus the proposed focus "has to be an enduring, government priority backed by resources and an intelligent plan." In Lesson 2, he observes that "if I, as premier, did not take a personal and active interest in driving academic achievement, progress would come to a halt."

He doesn't mean that he goes it alone. Resolute leadership means building the guiding coalition, the core group whose members meet frequently around purpose, progress, and corrective action and are always on the same page even when

Exhibit 4.1 Eight Lessons: Whole-System Reform

Lesson 1. The drive to make progress in our schools can't be a fad.

Lesson 2. Education reform is not important to your government unless it's important to the head of your government—personally.

Lesson 3. You won't get results unless teachers are onside.

Lesson 4. To succeed you need to build capacity.

Lesson 5. Settle on a few priorities and pursue them relentlessly.

Lesson 6. Once you start making progress, you've got permission to invest more.

Lesson 7. You're never done.

Lesson 8. The best way to sustain your effort to improve schools is to keep it personal.

Source: McGuinty, 2010.

there is disagreement. In the case of Ontario, the core team is the premier, the minister of education, the deputy minister of education (highest-ranking bureaucrat, equivalent of the state superintendent or commissioner), their policy staff, and me, as special advisor. Thus, resolute leadership becomes an organization or system phenomenon—literally, the organization pursues reform and its results relentlessly.

In Lesson 3, McGuinty notes that it doesn't matter how much money you spend or how much you want change, you have to figure out how to build a positive working relationship with teachers. This is not easy. Given the history that most teachers and their unions have had with past reforms, they are naturally guarded about the current ones. In effect, resolute state leaders say that we have to figure out how to trigger and reinforce the moral purpose and responsibility of teachers because we can't get whole-system reform without it.

Lesson 4 taps into another vein of wisdom for the effective resolute leader because it concerns the improvement of instruction. Capacity building, especially *collective* capacity building, is at the heart of successful whole-system reform. McGuinty puts it this way: "Sure, you can have world-class standards, rigorous testing and brilliant data management so we know precisely how each student is faring—but you still have to improve your teaching" (p. 6).

Lesson 5: Settle on a few priorities and pursue them relentlessly. Focus, focus, focus, and keep up the pressure and support—all the time. By this, McGuinty means that you must keep your eye on the ball, stay the course in this respect, and constantly be alert to deflecting distracters. Address distracters quickly and effectively so that the only real issue left is instruction and learning. Limit the number of priorities.

Lesson 6 captures the positive momentum of investing on top of success. It is necessary to kick-start the reform with new money (e.g., for capacity building). If you have the right strategy, you will get some success (within one year, in my experience). It doesn't take much success to legitimize additional budget. The public welcomes investment, provided that it is measurably paying off. In whole-system reform, success can be modest at times as long as it is steadily progressing.

Lesson 7: You're never done. McGuinty says that you need to be always learning and applying what you learn, going deeper in relation to what is working, and innovating for the next phase.

Finally, Lesson 8—keep it personal—makes sustained moral imperative a personal cause, a cause that you know can be accomplished only through connecting with others, drawing on and inspiring their moral actions.

What makes the Ontario story noteworthy, as does that of Finland, Singapore, and other successful societies, is not the actions of one person, but the way that leaders have combined the moral imperative and the focused action strategy to build realized moral purpose throughout the system at all levels. The essence of the Ontario strategy consists of direction and high expectations from the center coupled with a strong two-way partnership with the education sector that focuses on capacity building linked to results (for more elaborate analysis of the Ontario strategy, see Fullan, 2010a; Levin, 2008).

In particular, the strategy is based on eight interrelated components (see Exhibit 4.2).

Exhibit 4.2   Components of the Ontario Strategy

1. A small number of ambitious goals

2. A guiding coalition at the top

3. High standards and expectations

4. Investment in leadership and capacity building related to instruction

5. Mobilizing data and effective practices as a strategy for improvement

6. Intervention in a nonpunitive manner

7. Being vigilant about distracters

8. Being transparent, relentless, and increasingly challenging

In keeping with the first component, the initial focus was on literacy, numeracy, and high school graduation, with a clear target of raising the bar and lowering the gap in all disadvantaged groups. Literacy and numeracy were deeply defined to include higher-order competencies, and secondary school reform included innovations to personalize connections to students and to make programs more relevant to the life interests of students. These priorities have remained since the outset in 2003. In 2010, a fourth priority was added—early learning—which included beginning the provision for all four- and five-year-olds.

Second, from the beginning the leadership at the center, especially through the premier's personal presence, was seen as essential. As noted above, the premier chairs a group of leaders that includes the minister, the deputy minister, the chief academic officer, the premier's special adviser, and other policy people. This group, now called the Education Results Team, monitors progress, brainstorms on strategies, and basically helps the system stay the course relative to the core priorities.

Third, high standards and expectations are present in the ambitious targets that were set (going from 54% to 75% high proficiency in literacy and numeracy and from 68% to 85% in secondary school graduation). These goals were recognized as "stretch targets" and were treated as aspirational rather than as rigid outcomes.

Fourth, if there is one concept that captures the centerpiece of the Ontario strategy, it is capacity building. Major investments and strategies have been developed to build the capacity within the Ministry of Education to lead implementation of the priorities, especially in the creation of the Literacy Numeracy Secretariat (LNS). Similarly, support for and stimulation of instructional capacity and leadership at the district and schools levels has been the mainstay of the work of LNS in partnership with the schools and districts.

Fifth, when the strategy commenced, there was little capacity in the province to access data on results and practices. The arm's-length assessment agency, Education Quality and Accountability Office (EQAO), did collect and publish annual data on student achievement, but it was not organized for effective use. LNS created a data capacity based on EQAO data that is called Statistical Neighbours. This system is used both to stimulate improvement and to mark progress. In addition, LNS has coordinated strategies to access instructional practices that are associated with improvements. These strategies include the regular interaction between LNS teams and districts/schools, as well as a number of targeted strategies to get and spread effective practices.

Sixth, a key feature of the strategy was to encourage risk taking, learning, and sharing of successful practices while intervening in a nonpunitive manner. In other words, the strategy is deliberately light on judgment. Even the turnaround strategy, the Ontario Focused Intervention Partnership

(OFIP), strikes a positive tone as it identifies and helps struggling and stagnant schools and districts improve.

Seventh, from the very beginning we had a proactive mindset that distracters would be inevitable and that we would do our best to minimize their interference with the main priorities. A distracter is anything that takes away energy and focus from the core agenda. For example, continuous strife surrounding annual collective bargaining was a huge distracter in the period prior to 2003. The government made it a priority to establish four-year collective agreements with all unions. We are now in our second four-year agreement. Other distracters include ad hoc new priorities, excessive bureaucracy, and the like. It is not so much that distracters can always be eliminated, but rather that being vigilant about the core priorities is crucial.

Eighth, although the strategy is light on judgment, there are a number of aspects that increase pressure for accountability. These include transparency about results and practice, peer interaction and sharing across schools and districts, negotiation of targets and implementation plans between LNS and schools/districts, OFIP, and, more recently, new legislation that strengthens the expectation that school boards (trustees) have responsibility to focus on student achievement. More generally, the constant emphasis from the premier and the government on the core priorities keeps the Ontario strategy in the forefront at all times.

BECOMING "SUPERMAN"

I have spent some time in this chapter on the Ontario strategy because it is explicit, has a proven track record, and is a great large-scale example of the integration of moral purpose and strategy. The importance of this experience is highlighted, as I said earlier, by rapidly growing interest around the world in whole-system reform. The problem of lack of progress in many countries has become increasingly urgent especially since, in the case of the United States, the No Child Left

Behind goals in 2001 were so lofty and the movement so min-
iscule. Now there is Race to the Top, with well over $5 billion
being allocated to statewide reform.

The producers of *Waiting for "Superman"* quite rightly say
there is no superman that will save us. We need to start doing
the saving ourselves. This takes me to the third and final
"killer slide": Mutual allegiance and collaborative competition are an unbeatable combination—collective capacity full
blown. Anytime we have organized ourselves around the
moral imperative, and anytime we have furnished the action
means for people to focus together, build capacity, and get
results, two wonderful things happen: People become deeply
committed to each other (*mutual allegiance,* I call it); they really
do take pride in each other's success, and they are ready to
help. And they compete—with themselves and with each other.
They strive to do better for the common good. There are few
things more satisfying than the challenges and thrills of immers-
ing yourself in the Moral Olympics of making society better in
such a tangible manner as improving the life chances of scores
of kids while making the adults better at the same time.

What is really at stake here is the success of the nation.
Some countries—Finland, Singapore, South Korea, and to a
certain extent, Canada—have figured out that the quality of
the teaching force and moral purpose realized are *one and the
same*. In a recent report, McKinsey & Company (2010) investi-
gated the question of "closing the talent gap" by examining
the teaching profession in the United States and comparing it
to teaching in Finland, South Korea, and Singapore. In the latter countries, the teaching force is drawn from what McKinsey
called the 30+ group (the top 30% of university graduates plus
"suitability to teach" and providing good working conditions). In other words, 100% of teachers in the three countries
are drawn from the highest university ranks. In the United
States, the figure is 23% (14% in high-poverty schools). What
are the implications of the moral imperative realized for
addressing the 30+ problem?

McKinsey conducted some market research. Only 9% of top-third college graduates plan to go into teaching, so they asked a sample of the remaining 91% to compare teaching with their preferred occupation.

First, the question of money turns out to be somewhat confusing.

Interestingly, those who do not plan to go into teaching actually underestimate current teaching salaries (guessing that the current starting salary is $30,000 when it is actually $39,000). Certainly improving pay and the combination of financial incentives will be a necessary part of any solution (read the McKinsey report for several scenarios), but it will not carry the day. Let me put it this way (adapting Maurice Chevalier): "How are you going to keep them down on the farm once they have seen the farm"! To put it differently, there is no more powerful incentive than "moral purpose realized." When the 91% were asked about the most important job attributes they valued, the top ones were "the quality of co-workers, prestige, a challenging work environment, and high quality training" (p. 26)—the very factors that they perceived to be wanting in the teaching profession. It will be noted that these are some of the very qualities associated with actually accomplishing the moral imperative (as distinct from dreaming about it).

Becoming "Superman" requires creating dramatically better leadership and working conditions with associated capacity building prior to and during one's career. Some schools and districts, as we have seen in chapters two and three have managed to do this despite the current system. There is no better agenda, both in terms of values, and in terms of strategy and payoff than to take "realization" as the end game, and work backwards to create the conditions that will make it a reality across the whole system. It is not a mystery. We have seen clearly what it look like. The complexity is getting it to happen on a large scale. Realization is an if-you-build-it-they-will-come proposition. Moral exhortation is not going to change the quality of the teaching profession. Change the reality of teaching and word gets around rapidly and exponentially, I would pre-dict. It is going to require concerted and relentless effort implementing the set of ingredients that we have seen in this book. There are not that many factors at play, but they have to be there in chemical combination.

I have already stressed in the first paragraph of the preface that focusing on the actual accomplishment of moral purpose is the starting point. The moral imperative realized is absolutely crucial for whole system success in education which in turn dramatically feeds in the betterment of society and the world. One need only examine the work of health economists on the social consequences of unequal societies. Richard Wilkinson and Kate Pickett (2009) document in compelling and frightening detail how more equal societies almost always do better. We can take one of more than a dozen graphs presented by Wilkinson and Pickett. Exhibit 4.3 displays the relationship between income inequality and an index of health and social problems.

Exhibit 4.3	Health and Social Problems Are Closely Related to Inequality Among Rich Countries

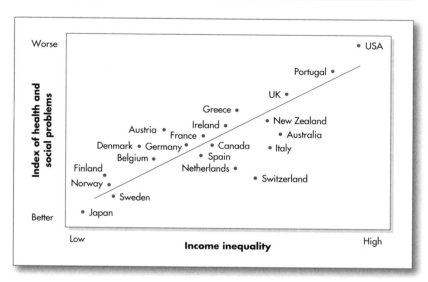

Source: Winkinson & Pickett, 2009, p. 20.

Income inequality is associated with lower levels of trust, more mental illness, lower life expectancy, obesity, teenage births, homicides, imprisonment, and a host of other societal and individual ills. Leaders with moral imperative know that improved education is one of the most powerful ways of combating these problems. While other policies are required to address welfare, housing, safety, and the like, educators who have experienced the power of *realized moral purpose* know specifically that education can make an immediate and lasting impact on the life chances of children and the quality of the entire society in which they live and, increasingly, in the global arena. Countries with better education make better neighbors.

What is especially noteworthy about the examples of realized moral purpose that we have seen in this book is that they (a) prove that it can be done, (b) tell us more precisely and specifically how it can be done, thereby being more usefully accessible to others, and (c) generate individual and collective energy the likes of which we have never seen (but only as a result of realization experiences). The imperative is an imperative only if we actually do it.

This takes us back to Nieman's (2009) intriguing observation that the opposite of doing good is not doing bad but rather good intentions that go unrealized. School and system leadership have now found a common niche. Leaders who get it know that intentions by themselves don't matter. Moral purpose, no matter how fervently held and expressed, is not a strategy.

Whether you are a teacher, a principal, a district leader, or a state or federal policymaker, the moral imperative boils down to one key factor—it is time to marry purpose and action. Make focused action with others your energizer. Above all, realize that you are in the business of actually improving lives and society—team up and be gratified by the fulfillment and be relentless in the face of the ever present challenges. The only thing that counts at the end of the day is *moral purpose realized.*

References

Bryk, A., & Schneider, B. (2002). *Trust in schools*. New York: Russell Sage.

Bryk, A., Sebring, P. B., Allensworth, E., Luppescu, S., & Easton, J. Q. (2010). *Organizing schools for improvement: Lessons from Chicago*. Chicago: University of Chicago Press.

Collins, J. (2001). *Good to great: Why some companies make the leap . . . and others don't*. New York: HarperCollins.

Dean, S. (in press). *Hearts and minds: A public school miracle*. Toronto, Ontario, Canada: Balboa Press.

DuFour, R., DuFour, R., Eaker, R., & Karhanek, G. (2010). *Raising the bar and closing the gap: Whatever it takes*. Bloomington, IN: Solution Tree.

Fullan, M. (2003). *Change forces with a vengeance*. London: Falmer.

Fullan, M. (2008). *The six secrets of change: What the best leaders do to help their organizations survive and thrive*. San Francisco: Jossey-Bass.

Fullan, M. (2010a). *All systems go*. Thousand Oaks, CA: Corwin.

Fullan, M. (2010b). *Motion leadership: The skinny on becoming change savvy*. Thousand Oaks, CA: Corwin.

Fullan, M. (2010c). *Motion leadership the movie*. [Online learning]. Salt Lake City, UT: School Improvement Network, and Thousand Oaks, CA: Corwin. Retrieved September 7, 2010, from http://www.corwin-sinet.com/Michael_Fullan_Info.cfm

Fullan, M. (in press). *The change leader*. San Francisco: Jossey-Bass.

Guggenheim, D. (Director). (2010). *Waiting for "Superman."* United States: Paramount Pictures http://www.waitingforsuperman.

Jackson, M. (2009). *Distracted: The erosion of attention and the coming of the dark age*. New York: Prometheus Books.

Johnson, D. (2009). *Ontario's best public schools, 2005/06: An update to Signposts of Success (2005).* Toronto, Ontario, Canada: C. D. Howe Institute.

Levin, B. (2008). *How to change 5,000 schools.* Cambridge, MA: Harvard Education Press.

Linton, C. (2011). *Equity 101.* Thousand Oaks, CA: Corwin.

McGuinty, D. (2010, September 13). *Lessons learned about whole system reform.* Keynote address presented at the Building Blocks for Education Reform Summit, Toronto, Ontario, Canada.

McKinsey & Company. (2010). *Closing the talent gap: Attracting and retaining top-third graduates to careers in teaching.* Washington, DC: Author.

Neiman, S. (2009). *Moral clarity: A guide for grown-up idealists.* Princeton, NJ: Princeton University Press.

Reeves, D. (in press). *Finding your leadership focus.* New York: Teachers College Press.

Seashore Louis, K., Leithwood, K., Wahlstrom, K., & Anderson, S. (2010). *Investigating the links to improved student learning.* New York: Wallace Foundation.

Sharratt, L., & Fullan, M. (2009). *Realization: The change imperative for deepening districtwide reform.* Thousand Oaks, CA: Corwin.

Wilkinson, R., & Pickett, R. (2009). *The spirit level: Why more equal societies almost always do better.* London: Allen P-Lane.

Yarrow, A. (2009). State of mind: America's teaching corps. *Education Week, 29*(8), 21–23.

Index

CORWIN
A SAGE Company

The Corwin logo—a raven striding across an open book—represents the union of courage and learning. Corwin is committed to improving education for all learners by publishing books and other professional development resources for those serving the field of PreK–12 education. By providing practical, hands-on materials, Corwin continues to carry out the promise of its motto: **"Helping Educators Do Their Work Better."**

The Ontario Principals' Council (OPC) is a voluntary association for principals and vice-principals in Ontario's public school system. We believe that exemplary leadership results in outstanding schools and improved student achievement. To this end, we foster quality leadership through world-class professional services and supports. As an ISO 9001 registered organization, we are committed to **"quality leadership—our principal product."**